BEHIND ENEMY LINES

For Dot

May God bless you
abundantly.
Please continue to
pray for those
persecuted for their
faith.
Paul
George

BEHIND ENEMY LINES

Gwynne Bounds
PIONEERS MINISTRY

SLAVIC GOSPEL ASSOCIATION
Eastbourne

DEDICATION

To Barbara,
the friend who would not allow me the luxury
of surrendering to discouragement
in the middle of this manuscript.

CONTENTS

PREFACE

IF YOU'RE ANYTHING LIKE ME, you'll be tempted to skip over this page. Please don't do that. This is the only opportunity I have to speak directly to you, the reader, about my reasons for writing these stories. It's important that you know.

Citizens of communist countries receive daily doses of hypnotism from infancy to death...it's called propaganda. By putting a practical application to Pavlov's theory of conditioned reflex, the message goes out via music, newspapers, books, TV, art, films etc., and obedient people receive the pleasant stimuli of material rewards, which in turn evokes the desired response of submission to the system. Troublemakers, and it must be understood that atheistic governments regard Christians as 'enemies of the state', receive less pleasant stimuli: intimidation, harassment, imprisonment or worse. It is not my purpose in this book to instil feelings of hostility in Westerners towards governments or people in Eastern Europe. Occasionally I've made some political comment, but my real purpose in writing these stories, is to share my own experiences of life under communism as gleaned from over twenty-five years of 'travellings oft' behind what Sir Winston Churchill called 'the Iron Curtain'.

In the first part of the book, it has been my aim to spotlight ordinary believers all over Eastern Europe. Not to put them up on a pedestal, but to show them as they are—people with problems, families with frustrations, churches having to make choices we know nothing about in the West. Christians in the communist world are not perfect, any more than we are; they do not live in a perpetual state of victory any more than we do; they haven't learned all the lessons there are to learn and they don't know all the answers. However, there is one very important area of the Christian life in which they can teach us a lot: they better understand what Jesus meant when He said, 'Take up your cross and follow me.' In countries where the official 'religion' is atheism, it *costs* something to be a believer in God. It costs some people their chance for higher education and a university place, even though they may be brilliant students; others may lose their jobs, their homes, their reputations, sometimes even their children and their freedom.

The last six chapters deal with the few weeks subsequent to 21 August 1968, when Czechoslovakia was invaded by Soviet troops and token detachments from four other Eastern bloc countries. I was there. I saw the tanks in the streets. I shared the disillusionment of my friends as their hopes for more freedom were dashed ruthlessly to the ground. But while the politicians were busy putting their house back in order, Christians were also busy trying to reach the maximum number of people for Christ, using the confusion all around them to their advantage.

I have also tried to explain some of the difficulties Westerners can experience in Eastern Europe. If you have never been behind the Iron Curtain yourself, you may have mental images of cloak-and-dagger operations. It's not like that. But at the same time, it is imperative to be 'wise as serpents and harmless as doves'.

Since the book deals with some subjects that are sensitive and current, a number of names of people and places have been changed. I do not want to hurt people or endanger the ministry of anyone—East European or Westerner—whom I respect and who might suffer if specific details were given. So, although all stories are true and all characters real, certain events have been related out of historical context in an attempt to further conceal identities of key people in the East. These, and only these, liberties have been taken.

I want to express my deepest appreciation to those who helped me write this book: travelling companions who patiently tried to remember details of trips we made together, with the hope that they'll forgive me for sometimes describing incidents of the occasion from my remembrance rather than theirs; friends who contacted me from time to time to enquire about my progress with the manuscript, offering steady support, wisdom and fresh motivation—even provocation!—in moments of discouragement and writer's block; my husband and others close to me who have often taken it upon themselves to do my household chores of shopping, meal preparation and even laundry so that I could have some uninterrupted writing hours...especially in the last few weeks before the completion of manuscript deadline arrived; and the members of our Sunday evening ladies Bible study group who have consistently supported and encouraged me with their prayers. I'm grateful to each one.

It is my prayer that after reading this book you will be more convinced than ever of the need to support missions such as the Slavic Gospel Association and the Pioneers Ministry, as they endeavour to 'Speak up for those who cannot speak for themselves' (Prov 31:8).

Gwynne Bounds
April 1989

FOREWORD

OVER THE YEARS many books have been written about the plight of the Christian Church in the USSR and Eastern Europe. Some have been useful and informative but not too easy to read. Others have tended to be melodramatic, exaggerated and lacking in balance.

When I was asked if I would consider 'Behind Enemy Lines' for publication, I was excited at the prospect. I have known the author for many years as part of a husband and wife team whose experience of ministry behind the iron curtain is second to none. Many teams and individuals have learned their skills from Brian and Gwynne Bounds of the PIONEERS ministry and wherever one travels in Eastern Europe they are held in high regard. Hints for prospective travellers are a novel feature included in this book.

Reading the manuscript it quickly became evident that this is a very 'readable' book. These are not just stories, they are personal experiences. This is not an account of what someone else has done. In every case the author was there at the time. This is an honest book. It talks of the frustrations as well as the joys. It sets nobody up on a pedestal and portrays the very human problems and difficulties experienced both by the ministering team and those to whom they go.

The message comes through loud and clear that there is

nothing glamorous about sitting for hours in a vehicle either travelling or simply waiting for something to happen. Waiting is a prominent feature of this kind of ministry and one which the traveller on the Lord's business must get used to.

The most important message of the book, however, is that this is God's work and we are but His instruments. *He* will finish the task. *He* will build His Church and *He* will glorify His Name.

Our prayer is that reading this book will not only be an interesting experience, but also a challenge to Christians to be available and be usable for the service of God.

BRIAN DINGLE
General Secretary
Slavic Gospel Association

PART ONE

1

GOD'S GUIDING ANGEL

WAS THIS ANOTHER one of my husband's jokes? If so, he soon found out that I was in no mood to be teased! After all, being cooped up for hours in an unventilated car at the top of a mountain, on the outskirts of a dirty Romanian village in the summertime, is not funny!

Not expecting to be gone long, Brian had left me there while he tried to locate a man named Lasku. We had never been in this part of Romania before and had only the pastor's name and the name of his village written on a torn scrap of brown paper. However, Brian was used to these assignments in Eastern Europe, so neither of us expected to encounter problems. But here he was now, hours later, hinting that he had been helped out of a difficult situation by an angel! From the reticent, and yet at the same time, animated way in which he talked, I couldn't tell whether he really believed his own story or whether perhaps he was just trying to smooth my 'ruffled feathers' with an unusual tale.

Let me backtrack a little and tell the whole story. The trip had been fraught with frustrations. We were travelling together with David, a Southern Baptist pastor and his wife. This was their first journey into Eastern Europe. The day we packed the car and set out from home we had actually intended taking them to Czechoslovakia, but Brian wasn't able to get a visa, so we headed the car in the opposite direction and took off for Romania. There was work to do in that country also. However, this change in plans cost us time. We had to buy extra provisions and supplies for a longer trip and also purchase items of equipment needed by the people we would be visiting. This delay was partly responsible for us arriving at the border between Hungary and Romania very late at night. There was no problem getting into the country; they just kept us there several hours for no apparent reason. We were more fortunate though than a young Englishman on a motor bike. He had been detained at the border for five hours even before we came on the scene and was still there when we left. The problem, apparently, was that he had grown a magnificent beard since his passport was issued. The border officials were insisting that he shave it off but he was just as adamant that he would not do that. I don't know what sort of deal he made with them or how much longer he had to wait at the border after we left, but we saw him in another town a few days later... beard in place!

From the border we drove to the first hotel we could find. 'We have no rooms,' the receptionist said nonchalantly. And her reply when we asked if she could suggest another hotel was a shrug of her young, boney shoulders.

Brian tried explaining that we were all very tired. 'It would be dangerous for us to try to drive further, after all, it's almost one o'clock in the morning,' he said pointing to the big round clock above the desk.

She wasn't impressed! It wasn't until he said that we would all come into the lobby and sleep on the couches that she became a little more helpful and looked again at the room plan.

'The only room I can offer you is a single room on the fifth floor. The lift is not working and you must be out of it

by six o'clock in the morning. A VIP is coming,' she said
with finality. At one o'clock in the morning my brain is not
at its best and it took me a little while to work out what a
VIP was.

'But even for that room, I must okay it with the man-
ager,' she continued, beginning to dial his number.

'But won't he already be asleep?' Brian asked.

'Yes!' For the first time we saw her smile. Actually, it
was more like a malicious grin.

When she put the phone down she was still amused.
Handing us the key she pointed us in the direction of the
stairs and continued her conversation with the dark young
man at her side. Since we would only have such a short
time in the small room, and because we would have to
walk up five flights of stairs, we decided not to bother with
luggage and night clothes. All we needed was our tooth-
brushes.

The single bed dominated the room and all of us agreed
that Brian should use it since he had done, and would
continue to do, all the driving. There was just enough floor
space for the rest of us to stretch out, but it was close
fellowship!

True to our promise we were out of the room by six
o'clock. There was no sign of the VIP. 'Well, David, that
was a good introduction to Eastern Europe, but you ain't
seen nothin' yet. The best is yet to come!' Brian *thought* he
was teasing the pastor.

We didn't have breakfast that day, so when, at about
eleven o'clock, we came across what looked like a public
barbecue and open air restaurant out in the middle of a
beautiful country area, we decided unanimously to stop
for an early lunch. We parked the car and mingled with
the locals, walking around the open fires and charcoal pits
to see what was available. Everyone seemed to be getting
the same: two thick slices of bread with what looked like a
hamburger between. We stood in line and accepted the

sheet of flimsy white paper handed to us by a gypsy boy; this was to serve as both serviette and plate. We then paid the number of lei the elderly woman with a metal cash box wrote down on a scrap of paper.

As we waited in line to get the food, David wondered aloud what kind of meat we were getting. Brian began to neigh like a horse and I bleated like a sheep. David didn't laugh. He turned pale. That was the first indication to us that he might be a finicky eater. Nevertheless, he accepted his 'hamburger' and followed us to a wooden table. It was filthy. We looked around for something cleaner but all the tables and benches were in the same state so the rest of us sat down. After thanking God quietly for the food, we began to eat. But not David. He just couldn't bring himself to even try it. Admittedly it was not up to McDonalds' standard, but it didn't taste that bad.

'Never mind, David, the best is yet to come and you ain't seen nothin' yet,' Brian joked again as we walked to the car.

David snacked on biscuits and crisps as we continued the long journey towards the town of Ploesti where we hoped to make contact with our good friend Josef. Arriving at his church in the evening, we were disappointed to learn from one of the deacons that Josef was conducting a wedding at a church in the mountains. The man wrote down the name of the town and Pastor Lasku's name. We found the place on the map—it was back in the direction we had just travelled...a long way back! There was nothing for it but to stay overnight somewhere and attempt to make contact the next day.

We are now at that July day I started to tell you about. Again the day began with frustrations. The hotel restaurant would not serve hot, black coffee. Instead they offered a lukewarm milky liquid with bits of skin floating on the surface. The bread was stale and the eggs were cold. The 'background' music attacked our sanity and the reluctant, cold-eyed waiters with inscrutable faces bypassed our table. These people had obviously never heard of the advertising slogan, 'Come to hospitable and romantic Romania'!

After paying the bill and evading those men with calculating minds who hung around the lobby quietly trying to entice us into changing money with them illegally, we set off on our journey. All went well until we turned off the main highway.

The mountain road appeared only on the map. In actual fact it was an unpaved dirt track of uneven ridges. There were no motorised tractors in these areas and private transport was non-existent. All ploughing was done by bullocks or horses. For over two hours we laboriously made our way through high-altitude farming communities, hoping we wouldn't break a spring or get stuck in a ditch. We also hoped it wouldn't be necessary to negotiate this road after dark.

Finally, we reached the village we were seeking. On the outskirts it looked quite small, just a few dilapidated cottages on either side of the narrow street. Brian searched for a place to park where we wouldn't be too conspicuous but the land was open pasture with no trees and consequently no shade.

It was mid-afternoon; the air was still and the street was deserted. I hoped it would remain that way as Brian told me to stay in the car with our daughter Wendy and David's wife, and to lock the doors while he and David went to make the contact.

I watched as they walked along the street and wondered how Brian would begin tracking down the pastor and Josef. Obviously we had prayed for God's help in this matter, asking Him for specific guidance, but when you don't speak the local language and you're eager not to attract attention to yourself, your options are limited. As they approached the fifth house an elderly peasant couple, both of them dressed in black from head to toe, came out from behind a high, tumbledown, wooden fence. I could see Brian showing them the piece of paper on which the name was written. They consulted with each other and somehow made him understand that he had to turn down one of the alleyways between the cottages. Without looking back at the car, Brian and David turned a corner and were out of sight.

For quite a while everything remained quiet and peaceful. It was easy to pray. But then things began to happen and people started to approach the car. We were gazed at by a young lad and sniffed at by his herd of filthy cattle. It was then that I closed the windows! About ten minutes later a suspicious, unsmiling, middle-aged woman sauntered slowly past the car. She was wearing black rubber boots up to her knees with dirty, faded overalls tucked in the tops and a red scarf tied tightly about her head and was leading dozens of noisy, smelly sheep and goats home after a day in the pastures. Word spread quickly. Soon the car was surrounded by scantily clad children all staring silently at us as though we had arrived from another world.

Finally, the sun dipped down behind the next mountain, the children moved back towards the village and we were left alone. At least it was cooler and we were able to open the windows again.

'Where can Brian be?' I murmured these words aloud. He had not expected to be very long and several hours had passed since I saw him turn that corner. Fears of impending disaster were hatching rapidly in the incubator of my mind and no matter how much I tried to keep my thoughts stayed on God, I could not find peace. For Wendy's sake, and because I knew that David's wife was frightened, I tried to stay calm but panic was growing. The 'what if's...' exerted themselves and bound my thought patterns.

The next hour passed very slowly. It began to get dark and I started to fret about the long drive down that treacherous mountain. Finally, through the gloom, I saw Brian and David come round the corner, their arms loaded with packages and their faces beaming. Naturally I was eager to hear their story, but because of my anxiety I greeted them with, 'Where on earth have you been all this time?' Furthermore, my rigid, straight-backed posture and glassy-eyed glare told my husband silently that I thought he ought to have been more considerate of us! But nothing seemed to deter his enthusiasm.

'When we turned that corner,' Brian said, pointing along the street, 'we climbed a little hill and I was absolutely horrified at what I saw. This is not a small village but a huge town! Within the space of three or four steps I stopped being optimistic and nonchalant about the task ahead and became realistic. Honestly, Gwynne, you wouldn't believe the size of this town. As I looked out over

that sea of red-roofed, ramshackle dwellings, I knew God was going to have to do the leading and be pretty specific about it if He wanted me to find Pastor Lasku and Josef. Humanly speaking it was impossible.'

Brian continued the story as we began our slow descent of that mountain. Occasionally David would interject a comment to clarify a point. Apparently, after pausing and praying desperately for guidance, they walked on and saw an old man leaning against a doorpost. Apart from him there had been no one else in sight, so Brian had shown him the dirty piece of brown paper with the name on it. He had squinted at it, but before he could say anything, Brian became aware of a younger man's voice saying, 'Folgen Sie mir nach!'—follow me! The young man had appeared from nowhere! How strange to hear German spoken in a non-Germanic part of the country! For over an hour Brian and David followed him down alleyways, through backyards and along main thoroughfares without speaking another word. Finally, the young man spoke again, 'Ihr Freund wohnt hier'—your friend lives here. While Brian looked around for the entrance in the high wooden fence, the young man went away.

'I'm not given to boasting about supernatural happenings every time something fantastic or unusual happens to us, Gwynne, but I feel quite sure that young man was an angel. He just disappeared from view. I never would have found that place if God had not sent a messenger from heaven to help me.'

There was an earnestness and a sincerity in my husband's voice that I had to acknowledge. Reluctantly, I had to accept his explanation. Nothing else made sense. But my feelings were still hurt about being left for so long, and my reply was, 'It's a good thing that angel wasn't delayed like the one coming to answer Daniel's prayer, otherwise who knows how long we would have been waiting on the top of that mountain!'

While David added a few thoughts and impressions of his own, he offered us food from the packages they had been carrying. I wasn't hungry but did sample one of the sweet cakes from the wedding reception while listening to David tell about their meeting with Pastor Lasku.

'Josef wasn't there. He had left about two hours before we arrived, so there was no one who could speak English,' he said.

'So what kept you?' I asked, still a little miffed at being kept waiting for so long.

'We went through the gate in the fence, and met a man. Brian showed him the piece of paper with the name on it and this brother beamed, pointing to himself to indicate that he was Pastor Lasku. Brian then put his hand on his heart, looked up to heaven and said, "Isus".' David started to cry. This surprised me. We waited for him to continue. 'I've never seen a man weep just at the mention of the Lord's name,' he whispered. 'That pastor cried as he repeated the word "Isus" with such love and adoration in his voice.'

David couldn't say any more so we drove on in silence for quite a while. Brian negotiated the tractor track expertly. In fact, we almost seemed to float down that mountain—no jerks or jolts and very few bumps. Each one of us was lost in our own thoughts...an angel unawares, speaking German, in a communist country. Obviously, when God sends His ministering angels out, He doesn't say, 'stop' at the Iron Curtain!

There were other occasions for Brian to tease David on that trip, but he was never able to say again, 'the best is yet to come.' None of us would have believed him.

2

VISIT TO THE FOREIGN MINISTRY

'WHY, OH WHY, did I choose to wear these high heels today?' I almost spoke these words out loud to myself as I clattered loudly down the long red marble corridor towards the two men who were waiting for me in the impressive Foreign Ministry building in Prague. I had wanted to give myself more confidence by looking smart but the noise of the little metal tips was making me nervous. I felt so small in this rather grand, high-ceilinged, palatial old building diagonally across the tree-lined square from the Prague Castle on Loretanske Street. Although I knew theoretically that the Lord was with me, I felt very much alone now.

The idea of coming here had been in my mind for a long time but I hadn't said anything to anyone about it, not even to Brian, and yet he was the reason for me being in this intimidating place now. 'Perhaps I should at least have informed the British Consulate of my plan,' I admitted to myself, but it was too late for that now. I had been brought to the Ministry by a Czech friend but even he had deserted me at the door. I didn't blame him. When you live in a country where the authorities assume that every foreigner from the West is a spy, he was right not to be seen helping me. But I didn't like being here by myself.

The portly security man at the door towered above me. I think he must have been deaf because he refused to acknowledge my presence until I raised my voice and almost shouted my question in his face. Even then he ignored me and walked away. Trying to give him the benefit of the doubt I thought perhaps he was going to look for an English-speaking-someone to help me. Instead, when he reached his desk he pointed to the wide staircase and turned his back on me. There was nothing for it but to climb the stairs to the first level and hope I would find someone there who would be more helpful.

When I reached the landing it divided into two long, high-domed corridors. Each corridor had rows of numbered doors on one side and long narrow windows on the other. The sun was shining through the dirty windows in the corridor to my right, so that was the one I decided to explore first. Outside each door there were two plain wooden chairs. For a moment I stood there wondering what to do. I was very nervous. My thoughts were in the form of a prayer but not one of my sentences was complete. However, since the Lord can see into our minds, He knew my fears, my questions, my needs and so I was trying to trust Him to somehow help me accomplish what I was here for.

Should I knock on a door? If so, which one? Should I wait for someone to come along and ask them if they spoke English? If so, how long would I have to wait? Should I go back downstairs to the security man and demand that he be more helpful? If so, how would I communicate with him? I had more or less decided to knock on the first door when another door farther down the corridor opened. Two men came out of the room talking and headed off in the other direction without even casting a glance in my direction. I ran after them and wished more than ever that my shoes didn't make so much noise. This place was so big and so quiet that they couldn't help but turn around to see who was daring to disturb the peace. As they waited for me to reach them they carried on talking to each other.

Neither one of them smiled; they just regarded me with impatience as I spoke to them in English. I felt like just one more interruption that neither one of them wanted to deal with but now I had someone's attention I wasn't going to lose them. Trying to practise positive love and appealing to their chivalry, I smiled and endeavoured to look helpless and in need.

'Do you speak English?' I tried to speak clearly and distinctly even though my heart was pounding inside my chest...and not just from running down the corridor either!

Neither one of them wanted to admit that he spoke English and by so doing they tried to rid themselves of the problem. Without saying anything to me they started to walk away but now my fear was spiked with a little anger. I was being ignored again. So I trotted along beside them. After a few steps, one of the men motioned to me that I should not follow them, but seeing the look of resolve on my face he must have realised that this red-haired 'problem' was not going to go away. He said something to his companion who carried on walking while he took hold of my arm and propelled me through one of the numbered wooden doors.

If I had felt intimidated out in the corridor it was nothing to what I now felt. The man let go of my arm, said a few words in Czech to someone sitting at a small desk far away on the other side of a huge room and left me standing there. Talk about passing the buck! I had just been dumped as another problem on someone else. Not knowing what else to do I made that long journey across the room to the desk and its occupant. The thickset, middle-aged man continued reading the document in his hands and refused to look at me. I didn't know whether to wait patiently or register impatience by beginning the conversation. I decided on the latter. To have stood there silently might have been interpreted correctly as nervousness and for some reason I remembered something Winston Churchill had said about dealing with communists. His appraisal had been, 'There is nothing they despise more than weakness and nothing they respect more than strength.' So once again I asked politely but firmly, 'Do you speak English?'

After a suitable delay, the man raised his eyes, but not his head, before getting up from his desk and indicating that I should follow him out of the room. He pointed to the chairs by the door and motioned that I should sit down. Now what? Had I been shunted off into another siding? Or was this man prepared to help me? Seeing no alternative at the moment, I sat down and waited. He returned to his room, closing the door impatiently behind him.

Fortunately, I didn't have to wait too long for someone to finally take an interest in helping me. The tall young man walked purposefully towards me, never taking his eyes off my face. After shaking hands, he asked why I was there. I explained that I was a British citizen with many friends in Czechoslovakia. 'In fact, my whole family loves your country very much,' I told him, 'but because my husband has not been granted a visa for over four years, we cannot travel to Prague together. I would like to know the reason for this denial and for you to tell me what can be done to change the situation.'

'Your husband must have done something illegal if he is an enemy of our state, otherwise he would not be refused a visa.'

'But I assure you, that's not true!'

'Please come with me. I will try to find someone who can give you information.'

We walked together, without speaking, into the other corridor, the one that was darker, and waited in silence for the lift to come. It was a rickety old thing, only big enough for four people to squeeze into, but since there was no one else present we could stand side by side without having to touch each other. The lift descended slowly, taking us to the first level below ground. Pulling the wooden swing-doors apart and clanking open the metal gate, we emerged to let others in.

There were no windows down here in the basement and the corridors were much narrower. The floor was concrete instead of marble and there was no colour anywhere. Everything was grey. The doors were painted grey; the light bulbs were grey with collected dust and the atmosphere was, generally speaking, dismal.

'Please write down your husband's full name on this piece of paper and wait here. I will return.'

The corridor opened out into a little waiting area. There were no chairs, no tables, no pictures or posters, just the bare concrete walls. It seemed an eternity until the young man returned but it was probably no more than ten minutes. While I stood there, people walked by and looked at me, but no one spoke to me. Finally, he called me into a room filled from floor to ceiling with rows of numbered and named files. By the door there was a small wooden desk and a barricade to prevent anyone getting to the files. The keeper of these files was a short, bald-headed man of about sixty. Standing straight and erect beside him was a well-built, dark-haired woman of about forty. She was obviously the senior of the two and was introduced to me by the young man before he left the room. She took control of the situation immediately by stating that my husband was 'persona non grata' in the Czechoslovak Socialist Republic.

From the impatient tone of her voice I knew I was going to have to work overtime to get this communist civil servant to help me. 'I understand that, but could you please tell me why?' I made my tone as soft and gentle as possible.

She opened the file that the little, bald-headed man put on the desk in front of her and flipped through several pages. If that was Brian's file, and it must have been because the woman referred to it in the ensuing conversation, I was amazed at how thick it was.

'Your husband was caught at one of our borders trying to bring forbidden foreign propaganda into our country. If I tried to do that at Dover I would also be refused permission to enter England,' she said.

I'm not much good at diplomacy but I knew I had to say or do something quickly to calm this woman down. She was about to close the file when I caught her eye and smiled. I didn't try to argue. I couldn't. After all, four years before, Brian and I had been travelling with another family to Czechoslovakia. We travelled in our separate cars. The other man had decided to attempt to take in Christian calendars that had been sent to him from Ecuador. There had been some discussion about the wisdom of this because the person in Ecuador had been evasive when we asked what he had said to his contact in Prague about the delivery of the calendars. Our policy had always been not to let anyone know our intentions prior to a trip to the East. We tried to find out with certainty whether or not any names had been mentioned in that letter and had been assured by the donor of the calendars that our identity had not been revealed. After the border incident, when the guards were obviously waiting for our group, we again contacted the person in Ecuador and he admitted that he had, in fact, mentioned specific names in his letter to Prague. He apologised for misleading us but gave the excuse that he thought we would not deliver the calendars if we had known the truth. He was right! As it was, they were not delivered and Brian's name was put on the blacklist along with that of his travelling companion.

'I know the incident you're referring to,' I said politely to the woman, 'but what I don't understand is why my name was not also placed on that list. I was with my husband on that occasion.' She read more details in the file.

Taking courage from the fact that she seemed interested in the case now, I continued, 'Although we were travelling with the other family, they were the ones with the calendars. Why should my husband be penalised for their actions?'

'There must be some other reason,' she muttered, still reading. Then after a slight pause, she continued, 'I don't make decisions. I only see that they are carried out.'

Her voice and attitude were beginning to get hard and cold again, so I hurried on, 'I do understand that you are not responsible for this barrier to my husband visiting your country, but could you please give me some advice as to who I should contact to try to get this ban lifted? I would be most grateful for any help you could give me.'

She started to interrupt me, but instead of cutting me off in mid-sentence, she seemed to change her attitude completely. Instead of terminating the interview in the negative way I expected, her words held some hope: 'You can tell your husband to apply again for a visa in one month.'

I could have hugged her! But from the way she closed the file and turned her back on me I was left in no doubt at all that our conversation was over. Right on cue, as though he had been listening at the keyhole, the young man was suddenly there to escort me out of the building.

Had I accomplished anything? Well, I succeeded in surprising Brian when I returned home and told him what I had done on his behalf. He was upset that I hadn't informed him of my intentions in advance. But when he was granted a visa the following month he thanked me for my action and finally admitted that he was very proud of me.

3

BULGARIAN HOUSE SEARCH

THIS STORY IS SET in Bulgaria and concerns a couple, Dmitri and Lidiya. We were not actually in Bulgaria when the events took place but were the first Westerners to visit Dmitri and Lidiya after they happened. Let me relate the story as they told it to us.

'Tell your parents to come to my office at eight o'clock in the morning.' The secret policeman spoke sharply to the two young boys who were standing close to each other in the kitchen of their home. Their parents were out at a meeting in a church a few miles away and the boys had not been able to prevent this policeman and his colleagues entering the small home when they had arrived thirty minutes after their parents' departure. It wasn't the first time the spotlessly clean, but austere, little apartment had been searched, but it was the first time the boys had witnessed such a thorough search. The brothers had to stand helplessly by as four policemen emptied cupboards, stripped beds, took up floor boards and confiscated things, and they themselves were watched silently and cynically by the two neighbours who had been commanded by one of the officers to come in as witnesses.

'Everything has to be done in a decent, orderly fashion,' the senior man had said with a sneer. 'We don't want your

parents accusing us of breaking the law, do we?' All the
adults had laughed.

The ordeal lasted two hours and although Dmitri and
Lidiya had told their sons to be in bed by nine o'clock,
Sergei and Alexei were still standing by the kitchen table,
viewing the chaos around them, when their parents
returned at ten o'clock. All their pent-up emotions
escaped as the door opened. They fled to their parents'
arms and sobbed. The sight was familiar to Dmitri and
Lidiya and it wasn't difficult for them to imagine the strain
their boys must have been under in the three hours they
had been absent.

Moving their sons slowly and gently towards the four
wooden chairs at the table, they sat down and listened to
the boys' story. All the religious books and Bibles that had
been carefully hidden in wardrobes and under floor boards
a few days previously had been found and confiscated.
Dmitri wondered whether this most recent house search
was triggered because the team delivering the literature
from the West had been followed from the border to their
apartment. It was a risk they always had to take. Dmitri
and his wife *were* prepared to take that risk, but they
didn't like their boys being affected like this.

As the boys told the story, their parents listened
patiently, only occasionally interrupting to ask a question
that would clarify things. As the boys talked, Lidiya began
slowly lifting clothes from the floor and folding them
neatly again while Dmitri read the list of confiscated items.
Their short-wave radio was gone and also their tape
recorder and cassettes. But the thing that upset Dmitri the
most, making him nervous, was the confiscation of his
little tattered notebook. He usually always kept this book
on his person, but had left the house in such a hurry that
evening that he had left it lying on his bed. He didn't think
the scripture verses and names listed there would mean
much to the secret police, but at the same time he didn't

want to underestimate their ability to break codes. How much information did they already possess? The code had been worked out in secret with a few Westerners who delivered literature to him regularly. They sent him postcards from scenic beauty spots all over Europe and always added a scripture verse in closing. Dmitri then knew when to expect the next delivery of literature.

When the boys finally finished recounting the events of the evening they prepared to go to bed. It was then that the sinister, underlying threat of this whole situation hit them. Sergei reached into his pocket and handed his father the card that the senior policeman had given him before leaving.

'Why did he give you this?'

'Because you and Mum have to go to his office early in the morning. But he also said there would be very serious repercussions if you did not report the next visit of Westerners immediately. And do you know what else they said, Daddy?' Sergei continued. 'One of the men put his arms around me and Alexei and said to the others that we shouldn't be saddled with old-fashioned parents who are "enemies of the state".'

Dmitri and Lidiya looked at each other. They knew what that meant. It was a veiled threat that the boys might be taken away from them and put in a state institution if they refused to co-operate with the police in future. Lidiya shuddered. Dmitri hugged both boys and praised them for their courage before praying a short prayer of thanks to God for His abiding presence and asking for a peaceful night's sleep for all of them.

Amazingly enough the boys did sleep but Dmitri and Lidiya talked long into the night as they tried to quietly put the kitchen-cum-living-room back to normal. 'What will you do, what will you say if they do threaten to take the boys from us?' Lidiya questioned her husband. 'Surely the Lord won't ask us to bear that cross.'

Dmitri didn't reply and Lidiya remembered the words of Jesus about loving father or mother, or anyone else more than God and therefore not being worthy to inherit the kingdom of heaven. She knew she wasn't prepared to make that sacrifice. Those Westerners would have to find other people to receive and distribute their literature. Surely Dmitri would feel the same way—but she didn't dare ask him. So when they finally went to bed, she lay there in the darkness wondering what they would be told at the police station, what threats would be made, what demands would be hurled at them.

All four of them were up early the next morning. Before the boys left for school they stood in the kitchen, holding hands with their parents and listening to their father's prayer. They wondered if he really felt as calm as he sounded. Lidiya wondered the same thing. She was nervous about their visit to the police station and didn't mind admitting it. But never in her wildest dreams could she have guessed what awaited them there.

They expected to be taken to separate rooms for questioning but instead they were escorted into a room containing a few chairs, a film screen and a projector. The windows were already darkened and the film began. *Ambassadors From Heaven* was the title.

After showing one or two churches with a few old people making an effort to sing, the scene moved to a border crossing. The guards were efficiently searching vehicles, going through luggage, taking off door panels and hub caps and discovering contraband material in Westerners' cars. The film was intended to be a comedy. It showed the futility of trying to 'smuggle' anything into Bulgaria and especially of risking arrest for the sake of a few old-fashioned religious books that very few people believed anyway. The half-hour film was made for TV and was due to be shown nationwide. It ended with a list of unpatriotic nationals who encouraged Westerners to bring in this unwanted, unneeded, anti-state literature. There were pictures of the people together with their names. To their amazement, there were their pictures and names on the screen. All the way through the film, Christians had been ridiculed and made to look idiotic. Now the sound-track was asking viewers to look out for these people and inform on them to the police if they were seen doing anything unusual... like carrying heavy packages to or from their homes, meeting with Westerners in parks or other open places, encouraging others, especially children, to go to church with them.

At that point, the lights were turned on and the inter-rogation began. It followed the usual pattern. They were separated, asked for the names of Westerners who regu-larly visited them, asked to whom they passed on their literature, where it was stored when it left their home, and when the next consignment was due. On and on it went. At first the interrogators were stern and loud. The second phase was more reasonable; Dmitri and Lidiya were both pleaded with to come to their senses, to see that their behaviour was only hurting themselves and their children. If they continued encouraging these deluded Westerners to break the laws of Bulgaria, they themselves would have to be punished and locked away from society, 'and then, what will happen to your boys?' they both were asked.

This was what Lidiya was dreading. Her boys were more important to her than the need to help Western missions bring in hundreds of pieces of literature so that they could make propaganda in their magazines about how much literature they had delivered and ask for more money to keep on doing the same. Her sons were both still young—twelve and ten—and their personal salvation and, therefore, her continued influence in their lives, was far more important to her than assisting foreigners in their ministries from abroad.

The interrogator seemed to know exactly what she was

thinking. 'It's all very well for these foreigners, they only have to get across the border with these books and then they can return to their bases with their glowing reports to their supporters about how brave they were and how their God helped them. But what about the risks you and your husband take? The actual distribution is the hard work. Just getting across the border is nothing. And as for their God helping them, they are stupid to think that they can get in with their cargoes unless we allow them to. We use them to lead us to people like you who are our enemies within our borders. They are so stupid when they think themselves clever.' The interrogator's contempt showed on his face as well as in his voice. 'We are prepared to give you a second chance to prove your loyalty to your country. All you have to do is report to us the next visit of Westerners to your home—whether or not they have literature. If you do that, you will be allowed to keep your children. However, if you refuse to co-operate, I will not be able to help you keep the boys at home. They will be taken away from you and put into a state institution. Think seriously about my words. These are not idle threats.' He paused for a moment and looked at her thoughtfully before saying, 'You may go.'

In a daze Lidiya looked around the corridors for any sign of Dmitri. Not finding him, she walked home and waited until he came. Lidiya had experienced two types of interrogation—the stern and the pleasant. Dmitri had been questioned three times. The third round had definitely been unpleasant. In their attempts to force him to agree to their demands, he had been beaten and the side of his face was now swollen and bruised from his fall against the table.

'What can we do? Did you agree to help them?' Lidiya was desperate.

'No, I didn't,' Dmitri replied.

'But what about their threat to take the boys from us?'
Lidiya was crying now and very distraught.

'We must trust the Lord. He won't allow anything to
happen unless it is according to His will for our lives. We
must not allow our faith in Him to waver, Lidiya. For the
boys' sakes we must be strong in our belief that God is
sovereign.'

She knew theoretically that her husband was correct,
but to put it into practice was more than she was able to do
at that point. Poor Lidiya. Dmitri hugged her and assured
her that everything would work out fine. She wanted to
believe it. She *desperately* wanted to believe it, but she
knew she would have to live on her husband's confidence
for a while. Seeing her picture on the screen and knowing
that the film was going to be shown all over the country
had come as a great shock to Lidiya. All their neighbours
would see it. Their sons' friends and their parents would
see it. Her family would be ridiculed and watched very
carefully by everyone wanting to keep in good standing
with the authorities. People might even be tempted to
make up stories about them in order to have something to
report. Oh, what a horrible nightmare.

It was two days later, very late one Friday night, when
we arrived on their doorstep. You can imagine our concern
as they shared their experiences with us. Could we trust
them? Would they report our visit to the police? Or would
their neighbours report our visit? If one of their neighbours did report our contact with Dmitri and Lidiya but
they themselves didn't report our visit they would get into
great trouble. The situation was serious.

Lidiya was the one who found a solution. She tried to
assure us of their love and continued friendship but suggested that we abort the rest of our trip and leave their
country immediately. She also suggested to Dmitri that
they should take the boys early the next morning and drive
out into a country district and stay there for the rest of the

weekend, arriving back in Sofia just in time for the boys to go to school and for Dmitri to go to work. That way, if someone did report our visit, they would have an excuse for not having gone to the police themselves.

We were grateful for this plan and promised to pray even more earnestly for them. We also agreed to their request that we let their other contacts in the West know about the recent developments and ask that no one visit them with literature for at least six months.

We did this, and most missions agreed to let their contact with Dmitri cool for a while. Just one or two individuals couldn't resist the urge to visit him in the hopes of getting an up-to-date story for their publications or prayer letters. Fortunately, no adverse effects of this were noticed. However, the stress and strain on Lidiya was very heavy. She became ill and very weak, and eventually died in 1975.

Her last words were, 'I'm just a passenger. I am going now to Jesus.'

Since she was the one in the family who had spoken good English, and communication with Dmitri was limited to 'God bless you' and 'Praise the Lord', some missions discontinued their visits to Dmitri and found other contacts. However, Dmitri maintained a strong witness and his commitment to the Lord's work never wavered.

Several years have passed since these happenings took place. We have kept in limited contact with Dmitri and the boys. On one occasion we arrived at their home and Dmitri, with his few words of English, profuse sign language and little drawings, made us understand that he had been expecting us. This surprised us since we had not sent a postcard or a message with some other team ahead of us to say that we were coming. Apparently, he had walked home from work, passed a tourist hotel in the centre of town and had seen our car. When we asked how he had known it was our car, he drew the car and wrote down the

Austrian licence number. He then drew other foreign cars with other number plates, giving them untidy interiors with monkeys and other things hanging in the windows. These other cars he crossed out and by our car placed a positive tick. 'God's car clean,' he said. Food for thought? Although we couldn't ever replace his notebook, we were able to take in a new radio, a new tape recorder and numerous cassettes of Christian music.

The most up-to-date news we have of Dmitri is that he is still serving the Lord and other missions, and is still suffering the consequences of these actions. The last time we saw him he had just been released from a spell in prison where he had been stripped naked, had a pistol held to his head and was threatened with death if he didn't give up his Christian beliefs and activities. He was accused of being a spy for America and the Netherlands and was the closest we've ever seen him to giving up. The authorities are still trying to break him and I'm left with the question, would I have fought on for so long if I had been in his situation? I honestly don't know.

4

CATHOLIC CHALLENGE

I'M ASHAMED TO SAY this, but I was twenty-nine years old before realising the truth that it is possible for a Roman Catholic to be a saved person. My bias in that area was not challenged until I met one very special priest in Czechoslovakia.

Friends of ours from America—also musicians—were travelling with us in Eastern Europe after having spent a few days in our home in Austria. It was fun making music together and even now, when we see each other, we reminisce about those days.

One Monday night we sang and spoke to a packed little Baptist church in the northern part of Czechoslovakia. Prior to the service, the pastor told us that the town's population had more than doubled recently. Apparently, the local army barracks on the outskirts of the town had been extended to house several thousand Soviet occupation troops. In fact, as we sat in the vestry, the noise of tanks clattering over the wet cobble-stones in the street outside was constant. Pastor Urban told us the manoeuvres would carry on right through the night. He was right.

The congregation was attentive, appreciative and

politely enthusiastic. In a quiet, reticent way, they communicated to us with their smiles that they were glad we were there. At the end of the service, when the last person had been hugged and we had received the last holy kiss, Pastor Urban invited us to have a cup of tea in his small apartment underneath the church. We gratefully accepted, looking forward to further fellowship with him and his family.

We spent that night in a small, misnamed hostel called 'The Palace Hotel'. Desiring to have more fellowship with Pastor Urban and his wife, we had agreed to accept their invitation for breakfast the next morning before leaving to drive on to our next meeting. Just as we were finishing a satisfying breakfast of brown bread, sliced ham and pickles, the doorbell rang loud and long. The pastor didn't move. A few minutes later his wife entered the kitchen and said something quietly in Czech. Quickly, the pastor left the room without saying a word to us.

After just a few minutes, he re-entered the small room with another man. My first impression of this other man was that he was agitated and anxious about something, but his beaming smile did not in any way project worry. He exuded excited anticipation.

'May I introduce the local Catholic priest? He wants to talk to you.'

Though surprised, we greeted him warmly and he came straight to the point. 'I've heard wonderful things about your service last night. You must also come to my church. It is the largest church in town. Please come tonight.'

What a shock! We were in Bohemia, not Yugoslavia, but this was definitely a 'Macedonian' call for help. Unfortunately we were expected in another town ninety-five miles away that evening, so it was impossible to accept his invitation. The man's disappointment was obvious and he wouldn't accept 'no' for an answer. 'If you can't come to the church tonight, then at least you must come to my home in one hour.'

We agreed, but for reasons of his own, Pastor Urban preferred not to accompany us to the parsonage. This didn't deter the priest. On receiving our promise to visit him in his home, the Revd Filipek left the house hurriedly. We assumed he was inviting us for coffee and fellowship. Imagine our surprise when we entered his living-room to find it filled with people of all ages. The priest had gone around the town inviting people to come and hear us sing and speak the riches of Christ.

The people got to their feet as we entered the room and the priest manoeuvred us through the bodies to the fireplace where he welcomed us briefly. Before taking his place by the door, he said, 'Now tell us what Jesus means to you.'

What an invitation! For one hour we sang and gave our testimonies. No one moved, no one spoke. Concentration was complete.

At 11.30 a.m. the priest dismissed everyone with the usual blessing. We were the only ones not making the sign of the cross. As one by one the people took their leave of us, there were many shared tears and kisses. When the room was finally empty, he began to share his testimony with us. Ten years earlier he had been imprisoned because his congregation was too large and his approach to the ministry was too evangelistic. All his teeth had been kicked out and many of his bones had been broken. But his spirit had remained strong and his faith had been renewed.

'When you have to go through treatment like that for your faith, all the trappings of religion fall by the wayside and only true faith remains,' he said thoughtfully.

I had to agree with him and silently wondered how much of my evangelical garb would have been shed under similar circumstances. Before leaving this man we prayed with him and promised to return to his church at some future date. Our promise was sincere but for some reason the Lord hindered Brian and me from keeping it. However, our American friends were allowed that privilege. They returned a few months later with a third musician to hold an evangelistic service in that Catholic church. Advertising was done by word of mouth. Some young people from the Baptist church, together with their pastor, went out on the streets, stirring interest by asking everyone they saw if they knew where the American group was 'performing'. This was a deliberate ploy and created an immediate curiosity in everyone's minds which wasn't satisfied until they knew the venue.

The huge church was packed with young and old. For three hours our friends sang, played their instruments—including the grand old pipe organ at the back of the church—gave their testimonies, preached the gospel and made an appeal before handing the service back to the priest. The people would not be dismissed, even though the church was bitterly cold. Again our friends explained what it means to be a true follower of Jesus Christ and still the people listened, hanging on to every word and every song. Finally, the Revd Filipek reluctantly pronounced the Benediction and some of the older people began to leave the church, but only after they had hugged our friends and showered them with tearful kisses. Most of the young people stayed for another two hours, asking questions that reflected the spiritual vacuum in their lives under communism. It was after midnight before the lights were finally extinguished and the last goodbye said. Father Filipek was overjoyed with the evening—so were our friends. So, too, was Pastor Urban who at first had been rather sceptical about the venture. Quite a few lives were changed by the Spirit of God that night.

The Revd Josef Filipek died the following year, so I never did get to see him again in Czechoslovakia. But I have no doubt we'll meet around the throne of God one day when denominational tags will be a thing of the past and the only thing that will matter is whether or not our names are written in the Lamb's Book of Life.

The Christlike Craftsman

A few years later I had the privilege to meet another priest in Czechoslovakia. He was not practising his vocation. This had been forbidden him by the communist government. He also had been in prison for his faith. I met him at his place of work—a glass-cutting factory. He was introduced to me as the finest glass-cutter in Bohemia. I was interested to find out how long he had been in the trade. Apparently, he had learned his craft while in prison and became so proficient in precision cutting that he was made to stay in the trade even upon release from prison.

'Even in confinement I tried to be true to the scripture that says, "Whatever your hand finds to do, do it heartily as unto the Lord",' he told me with a smile. 'I did not want to be in prison, but if God allowed it, who was I to argue? And while I would prefer to be serving God in the church, I continue to do my best for the Master in this factory. This is my place of service as long as He wills it and I know that He is the One who will reward me for my labours here on earth. So I must do my best for Him.'

That man's quiet acceptance of the destiny imposed on him by the godless, atheistic system of communism, ministered to me. I'm not sure that I would have shown such a Christlike attitude had I been in his position.

These two little stories have been included in this book because they are true. I leave them with you without further comment.

5

CAMEOS

SOMETIMES I FEEL as though our house is a revolving door! People coming, people leaving...tired people, happy people, nervous people, serious people...all on some kind of mission to Eastern Europe. Just like every other mother I try to be the hub of the wheel in my own family and, in addition, I endeavour to be a 'servant' to our visitors. This sometimes brings pressures and tensions I could well do without. But in comparison to my East European contemporaries, my problems are minute.

Consider for a moment what it would be like if, just as you are getting your children to bed, four strangers arrive at your home speaking a language you do not understand. They obviously want to come into your house and you assume they are here to speak with your husband who is a busy pastor and not at home at the moment. You show them into your living-room and with sign language try to explain that you must put the children to bed. Once the children are tucked away, you take a pot of tea to the foreigners and, pointing to your watch, try to make clear to them at what time you expect your husband to return. You're not sure they understand.

You're tired. You were looking forward to having a nice hot bath and going to bed early. There is still an hour before you expect your husband home and you know he would wish you to give the visitors some refreshment. But with very limited refrigeration, what can you serve? You have a few potatoes and some eggs. Apart from bread, that's all you have in the house. You have to shop every day for fresh produce and dairy foods.

I have to admit (reluctantly) that I've done enough moaning in my time about people who just arrive at my home without notice and expect me to produce a meal within thirty minutes. But look what I have at my disposal: a large refrigerator, a well-stocked freezer, cupboards filled with all sorts of conveniently packaged provisions and tinned foods ready to be prepared at a moment's notice. How dare I complain!

Well, my mother always used to say that confession is good for the soul, so now that I've shown you a somewhat unlovely, yet honest, portrait of myself, let me get on with the rest of this chapter by painting little pictures of very special, but more often than not, anonymous people.

At Home in Heaven

A short time ago an elderly brother with Bibles and other Christian books in his pockets dropped down dead on a street in Czechoslovakia. The police scornfully told the widow that since her husband had obviously been an 'enemy of the state' she would never know where he was buried. When she told them that such words could not hurt her because she knew her husband was with the Lord already, they were robbed of their incentive to terrorise her.

Parcel Post

There is one Lutheran pastor in Eastern Europe whom we always visit under cover of darkness. He and his family are constantly under surveillance. Without the aid of car lights we drive quickly into his yard, closing the rusty iron gate carefully behind us. The things we unload on to their living-room floor are not contraband, just a sizeable amount of new children's clothing, chocolate, small toys, batteries, plasters, aspirins, baby creams and lotions etc., plus brown wrapping paper and string. This quiet, unassuming elderly couple live in a small village and, in addition to their pastoral duties, they have a ministry of sending parcels to needy families in the Soviet Union. In a very real sense, this is an 'underground' ministry because no one in their church is aware of it.

Every time we visit this couple we are treated to rare blessings. The wife is an effervescent lady, always ready with an up-to-the-moment story of answered prayer. On one occasion she showed us photographs she had received from a very poor prisoner's family in Siberia. The jigsaw puzzles, dolls and toy cars we had taken on our last visit in the summertime had arrived at this family's home just in time for Christmas. We saw the children dressed in their new clothes and holding their treasured toys. God's timing had been perfect!

She even told us that as a result of another parcel, an alcoholic father had been converted. His children were constantly being ridiculed by their atheist teachers for being old fashioned in everything from their clothes to their mother's religion. The mother had no resources of her own from which to provide new warm clothes for her children as winter approached, so all she could do was pray and ask God to somehow provide. After receiving a parcel, they became the best-dressed children in school and their father felt ashamed and convicted—the result was his conversion.

Peer Pressure

It's sometimes true that the children of believers in the East have just as heavy a cross to bear as their parents. Not too long ago schoolchildren in Romania were given the following questionnaire to answer:

- How do you spend your free time on Sundays?
- Do you listen to religious broadcasts on the radio? What do you think of them?
- Do you go to church? What denomination is it?
- Who leads you there and who teaches you? Write down the name(s).
- What do you learn there? Are you told to pass on to others what you hear?
- What is a Christian?
- Where do you meet and how long do the meetings last?
- Do all members of your family share your religious convictions?
- Can you name other pupils in this school who go to church?
- Do you receive special literature at church?

Although in theory the replies to this questionnaire were supposed to be anonymous, it was clear that in some cases individuals were identified and exposed to ridicule. In fact, in one classroom, the teacher collected the answers and immediately took the paper of a twelve-year-old pastor's daughter and read it aloud to the class. She was mocked by the other students and reduced to tears. How would your children stand up to peer pressure in the form of derision?

Table-talk

Is a kitchen table as important as a Bible?

For years now Brian and I have been involved in a ministry of 'helps' to believers in the communist world. We enjoy putting 'tools' into the hands of East European Christians so that they can be more effective in reaching their fellow countrymen for Christ. This sometimes means providing cars for pastors who have the oversight of several churches. It can also mean supplying musical instruments to a church orchestra, or theological books to preachers, Sunday school materials, tents and sleeping-bags for summer youth camps...all very practical and obviously worthwhile needs. But what about a kitchen table? If you needed a small, formica-top kitchen table you could probably go to umpteen places in your home town to get one, couldn't you? Not so in Hungary.

When a schoolteacher friend of ours moved from one-room living accommodation to a three-roomed government apartment, she tried for weeks to find this mundane commodity. She even asked all her high school students to keep their eyes open but, apparently, kitchen tables were unobtainable at that time in Hungary.

Now perhaps you're thinking that a table is a strange secular need that could well be left unfulfilled when there are so many other spiritual necessities. But wait! This teacher has a ministry to her students in her home. It's forbidden for her to spread her Christian beliefs in the class-room, but in her own home she's free to share her faith. Her vision was to invite the students in small groups to her home, and by saying a short prayer of thanksgiving before the meal, give them an immediate opportunity to question her about her faith—but she was hindered because she had no table.

I'm happy to say that within a very short period of time we were able to supply her not only with a table but also a refrigerator. So her evangelistic outreach is now in full swing.

Testimony to the Troops

When the Russians invaded Czechoslovakia in 1968, the majority of Czechs felt that they had been stabbed in the back by their socialist brother. Consequently, once the argumentative dialogue with the soldiers on the streets ended, most Czechoslovak citizens made their protests silently by turning their backs whenever occupation troops came into sight and by refusing to speak to any foreign soldier.

There was one notable exception! Our friend, Ivan. He would walk into the army barracks with his pockets and brief-case full of Bibles and New Testaments. His contagious smile attracted the young men who had quickly become disillusioned by the 'cold shoulder' effect on the streets. After all, they had been told in their pre-invasion briefings that they would be welcomed as heroes in Prague. But they had experienced only contempt and outright hostility. Ivan would sit and talk with these fellows and, following Jesus' example, be a friend to sinners.

In February 1969, six months after the invasion, Ivan dictated a letter to me at his home in Prague. I didn't take down his words verbatim, partly because we could have been searched at the border when leaving the country, but mainly because Ivan's speech was a mishmash of German and seventeenth-century English—he had taught himself English by reading the Bible...a King James Bible!

At the conclusion of his letter he said, 'I praise the Lord that He has enabled me in the last few months to travel over 35,000 kilometers in my own country...to conduct more than 277 preaching services...to minister regularly in three churches...to lead 70 souls to the Lord Jesus, but one of my greatest joys in 1968 was to give more than 600 Russian Bibles and 2,000 Russian New Testaments with Psalms to the Russian troops stationed in our land. Please pray that these boys might find Christ in our country.'

One year later a police interrogator in Prague asked Ivan how many Bibles and New Testaments he had handed out to Russian soldiers. Ivan said he didn't know, but however many it was, it wasn't enough. The policeman opened a drawer in his desk and took out a copy of Ivan's letter. 'Refresh your memory,' he said harshly, handing Ivan the letter.

Since I had drafted, typed and posted the letter in

Austria, Ivan had never seen a copy of his letter. How the police in Prague got a hold of one, none of us will ever know. That letter was only posted to thirty-five of Ivan's closest friends in the West. Makes you think!

Compromise or Conviction?

Basically, there are three types of pastor in Eastern Europe: those who make concessions and agree to a little compromise with the communist authorities in order for them to be allowed to continue their pastoral and preaching duties; those who refuse to collaborate in any way by saying in effect, 'my business is spiritual, your business is political—you do your job and I'll do mine'; and the fighters—those who refuse to inform and who speak out boldly about the injustices of communism and the lack of religious freedom.

Now I have to be careful here. I'm not throwing stones or being critical of the first type of pastor. His motive is often honourable. He reasons with his conscience, 'If I agree to these small requests for co-operation, I'm not committing a sin and what harm does it do to keep records of how many people are in church each Sunday or to obtain prior permission for a visiting speaker to preach? By doing that, I am guaranteed the right to continue pastoring my church. I may even be given permission to attend conferences abroad.'

However, what usually happens to this man is that the 'little' requests for co-operation gradually develop into full-blown compromise demands. Finally, his conscience (unless it is seared) won't allow him to comply with the demands for more and more information about the people attending his church and the Westerners who visit him. This is a real dilemma. If he refuses continued co-operation with the government, the result will almost certainly be a rescinding of his preaching licence, maybe even imprisonment. If, however, he continues the alliance he will gradually lose the respect and trust of his congregation. Either way, he loses. Some choose the first option, others go with the second.

The second of our three types of pastor just wants to be left alone to get on with his job. But the communists will try many tactics to bring him into line. Often you will find that this man is given godly wisdom and holy boldness when called in for questioning. For instance, a friend of ours had angered the local authorities by allowing an American evangelist to speak in his church without pre-registering him with the police. The visitor had arrived at the pastor's house unexpectedly one Saturday night. Without hesitation he agreed to the pastor's request that he bring a three-point greeting (another way of saying 'sermon') the following day at church. The official informer in the congregation—and there's always at least one—reported this to the police on the Monday. Our friend was called in to explain the absence of his report on this matter on the Wednesday.

'You know you are required to obtain advance permission for foreigners speak in your church. Why didn't you do this?' the police chief shouted.

'But I love my country,' our friend replied quietly. 'How could I say to an American that he couldn't speak in my church. He might have said to me, "But I thought you had religious freedom here." I would not want to put my country in a bad light to a capitalist, would I?'

The policeman had no reply. What the Bible says is true, 'A gentle answer turns away wrath' (Prov 15:1).

The third type of pastor mentioned above cannot be tolerated indefinitely by the communists. They are labelled 'enemies of the state' because they dare to defy and argue and usually end up in prison, being deported or having their preaching licence taken away. Their consciences are clear before the Lord but their ministry in their homeland is usually terminated. Of course, there are exceptions. I'm not making hard-and-fast rules here.

This is a very complex subject and it would take a whole book to cover the topic. But since Western missionaries travelling to the East must, of necessity, raise such question as 'Who can be trusted?' or 'Of whom should we be careful?', I thought you ought also to be confronted with these problems in order for you to understandingly pray for all involved. Both the pastors who experience the pressure of living and working for the Lord in an atheistic environment, and Western missionaries trying to assist them in their task of reaching their own people for Christ need prayerful support.

Wisdom in Action

When a group of Romanian pastors from several denominations bravely signed a document exposing the denial of basic human rights in their country, it was not long before each one of them was called to the police headquarters for questioning. They were interrogated separately for many hours and threatened with beatings. In fact, at least two of the men were hit by angry interrogators. The oldest pastor of the group, a godly Pentecostal pastor, knew that his fellow ministers were under tremendous pressure, so when his turn came, he asked the policeman to be kind enough to introduce him to the man who would have to beat him. The pastor explained that he was an old man and had a weak heart. Therefore, he wanted to pray for the man who would beat him because that person might be responsible for sending him into eternity. He was not beaten!

6

RAGS TO RICHES

WHENEVER WE VISITED the church in Jablonec, Martina and Jan always asked us to stay in their home. They didn't really have room for us. But they were prepared to put up with even more inconvenience than normal, if only we would stay with them. Their three-roomed dwelling was very dilapidated and very crowded. In addition to their two small daughters and a cat, Martina's elderly parents also lived in that house.

Communication with the family was a little complicated. The grandparents only spoke Czech, as did the two little girls; Jan and Martina communicated with each other in Hungarian; we talked to Martina in English and Jan in German which had to be translated into the other language for each one of them and into Czech for the children and grandparents. It's little wonder that our conversations went on into the small hours of each night whenever we were there!

Jan was a tall young man, his back straight as a rod. When he stood at the rear of the church with the other young men, he seemed to tower head and shoulders above them and be just a little aloof. Martina, on the other hand, was petite, had beautiful black hair, but it was her eyes above all that distinguished her from the other young women in the stringed orchestra. At one moment they seemed to be hazel, though flecked with green and blue around the irises; a moment later, with a change of light, or perhaps a change in her mood, they were an astonishing violet, and they always sparkled.

Our visits to their home followed the same pattern each time. As soon as the service in the little church was over, Brian and I would stay behind to talk to everyone, but Wendy would go home with the family. Then by the time we arrived at their home there would be the usual chunks of brown bread and home-made sausage on the table, together with lukewarm mugs of sweetened lemon tea. After eating, grandparents and children would go to bed in one room and the four of us would settle back and enjoy each other's company in the kitchen.

The conversation between Brian and Jan took the same form each time we visited. Jan was Hungarian and came from a strict Roman Catholic family. He would tell Brian that even though he always went with Martina to the Baptist church, he was never able to fully believe the 'Baptist Creed'. By that he meant he could not say with certainty that he was going to heaven when he died. 'The Baptists are egotistical when they say they *know* they will go to heaven,' he would say over and over again.

Brian would try to patiently show him from the scriptures that it is possible to know assurance of salvation and that justification comes only through faith and not through good works. 'This is not the Baptist Creed, it is God's word.' Jan wanted to believe and was always reluctant for Brian to stop talking to him. We prayed very much for Jan and that family, fully believing that God would answer our prayers and that one day we would all be able to rejoice in Jan's salvation.

It wasn't until about the fourth visit to their home that Jan shared his secret with us. When the children and the grandparents were in bed he asked Martina to get two boxes from their hiding place. No amount of imagination could have prepared us for this couple's secret. They were titled people with a vast inheritance waiting for them in West Germany! Apparently, when Jan's parents were divorced, he had gone to live with his mother in Czechoslovakia and his father had remained in Hungary. Sometime later Jan's uncle and father had transferred the family's wealth to Bavaria. Jan was an only child. His father had died. He had inherited the title and family fortune. It was all very impressive and all very secretive.

For hours we looked at family photograph albums of Jan's relatives and ancestors. His family had obviously been very important, wealthy people in the Austro-Hungarian Empire. Their family homes were manor houses and their estates were vast. The wedding pictures showed family members on horseback in splendid uniforms. We could hardly believe what we were seeing and hearing. All the more so, when, before going to bed, we were brought back to the reality of the present by having to put on our coats and boots, walk down the alleyway behind their house and across an open piece of land to get to the very public, very smelly convenience. What a misnomer! There was nothing convenient about it!

The next morning Jan said goodbye to us before riding his old black bicycle to the factory where he made fire extinguishers. He promised to tell us more of his family history after the meeting that night, but cautioned us not to say anything to anybody about the privileged communication we had received the previous night. We promised.

As you can perhaps imagine, we felt entrusted with a gold mine of information and I could hardly wait for the service to be over so that we could huddle around the little stove in their kitchen to hear more. I'm a romantic at heart!

Jan seemed somewhat reluctant to begin the conversation though. Perhaps he regretted having shared his secret. Brian sensed this and assured them both that their confidence was safe with us. If they didn't want to tell us more, we would understand.

Jan seemed to weigh up these words before speaking. 'Well, you already know most of the story, but now I want to show you my castle in Bavaria. It is ready and prepared, just waiting for us to take up residence.' With those words he showed us a black-and-white photograph of a beautiful old castle, set in a wooded area and surrounded by a moat.

'It is not far from where you live,' he told us. 'We want you to come and visit us there.' He waited for our reaction. Brian and I looked at each other in stunned silence. This was a really big secret they were sharing with us.

'You mean you're planning to leave Czechoslovakia? When? How? Legally, or by escaping? The whole family?' Oh, we had so many questions.

The next two hours were spent listening to their plans. No one, not even Martina's parents, knew of their intentions. How humbled we felt to be trusted with this information.

Martina and Jan did leave Czechoslovakia with their two daughters and one of the first telephone calls from their castle was to us, begging us to visit them the following Saturday afternoon. They gave us directions to their village and told us we would have no difficulty locating their new home once we were in the area!

We really felt an excitement as we made the two-hour journey through southern Germany. Wendy wanted to know if they would have servants and if there was a drawbridge over the moat. Brian joked that Jan was probably driving a big black Mercedes now instead of riding his ramshackle old bike. I wondered how we should address them in front of others. They would always be Jan and Martina to us, but we wouldn't want to be disrespectful to them when others were present. And the overriding question was 'Will they be happy with their new life?'

Sure enough, it wasn't difficult to spot the castle. It looked just as we remembered it from the tattered photograph we had seen in Czechoslovakia. We left the country lane and drove through the huge wrought iron gates at the edge of their property and on down a wooded drive before crossing a narrow bridge over the moat. There, in the inner courtyard of the castle grounds, next to a fountain, was—you guessed it!—a brand new, black Mercedes. Before we could get out of our car, Martina came running nimbly across the cobbles to greet us. After hugging each of us in turn she apologised that Jan was not there to greet us, explaining that he was interviewing a local man for the position of gamekeeper and would join us as soon as possible. 'Let me show you around. Wendy can play with the girls while we explore. We'll have coffee later.'

The next hour was spent wandering along marble corridors, admiring huge paintings, touching suites of armour, sitting on antique furniture and praying together in the ornate private chapel. Finally we arrived back at our starting-point in the one wing of the castle that was heated and habitable. Martina made coffee and served us home-made cake. No, she did not have servants.

'You can't imagine how wonderful this is for me to have a proper kitchen with hot and cold water and even a washing machine! I couldn't stand the thought of anyone else working here. This is my home,' she explained. 'And anyway, I've always done my own work. Why should I pay anyone else to do what I enjoy doing for my family?'

A little later in the conversation she explained that Jan's uncle had tried to insist that she employ a couple of local women to do the housework and cooking. 'He's upset with me and thinks I'm stubborn, but what would I do with my time? In fact, I told him I could take in washing from the village folk because I have a beautiful big washing machine and lots of hot water. He won't let me,' she said.

As Brian and I drove home that evening after spending

several hours with Martina and just a small amount of time with Jan, we were disturbed. It was true that they had only been in the West a short time and that Martina didn't speak much German yet, but they hadn't done anything about finding a church home. Instead, 'Uncle' had arranged for the local priest to come to the private chapel to say Mass each Sunday. Martina seemed to miss the fellowship but Jan had little interest in doing anything his uncle would frown upon. And, from our brief encounter with Jan's aristocratic and autocratic uncle, it was clearly apparent that he didn't wish his nephew to mix with Protestants. He was taking it upon himself to teach Jan, who in turn tried to educate Martina and the children, to think and behave in a way befitting their titles, Count and Countess von Rostotsky.

The next time we went to the castle, Martina's parents were visiting from Jablonec. They cried when they saw us and although we couldn't understand the words they were saying, we understood their meaning very well. These poor, lovely people were distressed at what they saw and felt in their daughter's family.

Not long after the grandparents returned to Czechoslovakia Martina telephoned us to say, sadly, that she was leaving Jan. She explained that he had a mistress; the money and position had gone to his head and she, together with the children were in his way. He felt she was holding him back from the pleasure that he deserved and she couldn't adapt to his way of life. We prayed with her on the telephone and promised to visit her in the little apartment she was renting for herself and the children. 'This is one Countess who may have to take in washing to earn a living,' she said with a shallow laugh just before hanging up.

Jan is still in his castle managing the huge estate and brewery. Martina still has her title and her faith—but that's about all. She's separated from her parents by an impassable border. No way could she ever return to her family and friends in Jablonec.

Not every story about East European believers has a happy ending.

7

A DREAM COMES TRUE

DO YOU BELIEVE GOD can speak through dreams today? If anyone had asked me that question a few years ago I would probably have laughed and dismissed the subject by saying He has no reason to. Now, I'm not so sure. Something happened in a remote part of Eastern Europe to make me change my mind.

Our assignment was to visit a Christian family we'd never met before, in a place we'd never travelled to before and no one could give us their complete address—it was another one of those assignments where we knew only the name of the family and the name of their village. It was essential for us to make contact with the father and deliver a large amount of money to him for distribution to needy believers in this remote part of rural Romania. We were told that the man was a trusted lay preacher; trusted by the believers not to compromise with the secret police and trusted by Western missions to distribute finances wisely and sensitively to those in need.

This story takes place on a lonely stretch of country road. The village we were searching for seemed to appear only on the map. Eventually a dilapidated sign, almost completely obscured by untidy roadside trees, announced the boundary line of the community. Slowing down and peering into the driving rain we searched in vain for any evidence of life. It was only seven o'clock in the evening but the darkness was already intact and pure. There were no street lights, no lighted windows, not even the flicker of candlelight or the subdued glow of a lighted cigarette. Nothing.

Driving almost at stalling speed, it only took three minutes to reach the other end of the village, so making a three-point turn Brian headed the car back along the deserted street in the opposite direction. This time I noticed a solitary figure lingering in the shadows of the tall grass and shrubs at the side of the road. In fact, all three of us in the car saw him and all three of us instantly recognised the unmistakable uniform of a communist policeman. We had almost made the mistake of stopping to ask directions but instinctively we knew that our British practice of regarding policemen as friends could not be applied in Romania.

Picking up speed slightly Brian drove to the last house of the community, and noticing a small side road to the right quickly turned in. By this time we were all talking at once, not only to each other but in a naturally urgent way to God asking Him for clear and quick guidance. If that upholder of communist law was looking for stars on his cap or even something to relieve his boredom in this sleepy little hamlet, he was probably already making his best speed towards this end of town. In a country where 'Big Brother' is alive, well and active, no unusual activity is dismissed as insignificant. So to this constable, a foreign car cruising slowly through his territory would be interesting; a foreign car stopping in his territory would be provocative.

There was a slight left-hand bend in the road and as we rounded this curve we saw a dim, solitary light bulb shining through the darkness over a green wooden door at the very end of the street. This pale light was like a beacon to us. There was no question in any of our minds. If we wanted to find the family we were looking for we had to ask for directions at this house. There was no viable alternative. So Brian manoeuvred the car as close to the door as possible. Still in the shadows, he turned off the lights but kept the motor running. Our co-worker, Bill, got out of the car and made his way nimbly over muddy ruts in the unpaved street to the door.

Even before he had finished knocking, the door was opened by a dark-haired man. Without speaking, Bill handed him the scrap of paper on which someone in another town had written the name of the family we were trying to locate. The man read the name, opened the door a little wider and called some words over his shoulder, but never took his eyes off Bill. Within seconds a plump, curly-haired teenager wearing dark-rimmed glasses appeared. Hesitantly, and with great concentration, she spoke a few words of English.

Brian and I were practising the scriptural injunction to 'watch and pray'. He was watching through his rear-view mirror for any sign of that policeman and I was praying that the people at this house wouldn't waste time. The last thing we wanted was for that policeman to arrive on the scene. His questions would be difficult to answer. However, the girl's question was not difficult to reply to. 'Are you a believer?'

What a strange question. Bill assured her with a smile, folded his hands like children do when they're praying and gave a reverent look up to heaven, indicating that he was a Christian. 'We also.'

Could this be the family we were looking for? That would be a miracle. Almost too good to be true. Without speaking Bill pointed to the name on the paper and looked questioningly at the girl. 'We know them. I will take you to them.'

He urged her to hurry to the car but didn't say anything

to her about the policeman. Perhaps he was afraid she would change her mind if she knew the possibility of police attention. Pulling a dark coat around her shoulders, she slipped into some sturdy shoes and came towards the car. Slipping into the back seat beside me she immediately leaned forward to give Brian directions. I searched the darkness for any movement in the street behind us and seeing none, asked the Lord silently for His angelic protection to surround this home. Brian drove away without lights, following the girl's simple directions.

The road surface deteriorated rapidly the farther away we got from the main road until eventually we were squelching through mud baths. I was afraid we would get stuck and asked her how much farther we had to travel.

'Just one more corner.'

She was right. We rounded a sharp bend in a narrow street and there, waiting under the eaves of a single-storey dwelling, were five people. Our young friend indicated that we should stop the car because this was the family we wanted to meet.

Since they were obviously expecting us, I assumed that the dark-haired man had telephoned them, but reason quickly told me that these people didn't have telephones way out here in this rural backcountry. Why, then, were these people standing outside their home in the rain, all of them dressed in their Sunday-best clothes, just waiting?

Brian parked our car in their courtyard. The father closed the tall wooden gates behind us and motioned all of us towards the house. Our young teenage friend spoke hurriedly with the wife before shaking hands and saying a solemn goodbye to each one of us in turn. Brian tried to get her to understand that if she only would wait a while we would take her home again. That's how Western minds think. The father patiently explained to us that in their society it would be better for all concerned if she didn't

know any details of why we were there. She nodded her head vigorously in total agreement and left the house.

Once inside their kitchen my curiosity got the better of me. I had to find out why this family had been waiting outside their home when we arrived. Their story made no logical sense to me. Apparently, the wife had dreamed the night before that they were to receive a very large gift. She had been so convinced this was a message from the Lord that the whole family had changed their plans for the day. Instead of visiting friends as planned, they had dressed as if they were going to church and had waited patiently at home to receive their gift. When night-time came they had not become discouraged or even begun to doubt. Instead they had become more excited and animated, knowing they wouldn't have to wait too much longer. Finally, at seven o'clock, the father had suggested they should wait outside to welcome their gift when it arrived!

A phrase kept running through my mind as they spoke...'unless you become as little children....' Their faith was disarmingly childlike and in a way it unnerved me. I wasn't completely comfortable with this simple trust in a dream, but had to admit that a peaceful calm pervaded this home.

We had indeed brought them a large gift. More money than they could possibly have made in a lifetime of collective farm work. But none of us in the team had any hesitation handing it over to them. The wife took it, kissed the envelope with eyes raised towards heaven before hiding it in a sack of flour.

I just hope God never asks me to receive His instructions via a night-time vision. I'm not sure I would take Him seriously.

8

LEFT-HANDED SECRETS

THERE ARE SOME CHRISTIANS in this world who seem to be able to quote scripture verses for every occasion and situation. In a way this disturbs me and I'm not sure whether it's because I don't know the scriptures well enough myself to be able to do that, or perhaps because sometimes the quotes are delivered in an uncaring, dogmatic, 'take it or leave it' sort of way. For instance, the perfect verse to quote to the fearful old saint I'm about to tell you of would have been the one that says perfect love casts out fear; or perhaps the one that tells us that God has not given us the spirit of fear but of love, power and a sound mind. Or would those verses have been so perfect? Judge for yourself.

My husband told me this story following one of his trips to Romania. It was very late when Petru stopped his car at the end of a deserted, unpaved, narrow little street on the outskirts of Bucharest. There were no street lights and very little illumination from the moon. All windows were darkened and there was no sign of life anywhere.

'The old man's house is the fourth one on the left. Go through the gate and you will see his door straight in front of you. Go, and God be with you.'

'Are you not coming with me, Petru?'

'No, you must make this visit alone. Go now, I must drive on.'

'But where will I meet you afterwards?'

Brian was in an area of the city that he was not at all familiar with and he didn't really like the idea of being stranded out in the middle of nowhere so late at night.

'Don't worry! I will be waiting in the shadows. You won't see me but I will be watching out for you.'

There was no alternative but to trust Petru implicitly and to do as he said. So Brian got out of the car quickly, closing the door softly so as not to disturb the silence all around him. Petru drove his dark blue estate car slowly on, rounded the next corner and was out of sight. Brian was not really happy about making this visit alone. 'What if the man doesn't speak any English or German? How will I communicate with him?' These were questions he was asking himself but for which he had no answer. His purpose in making this contact was to deliver a financial gift from one of the old man's friends in America.

At the fourth house he went through the tall gate and there, in front of him, was the door. There was not even a faint glimmer of light from any window. Brian felt sure that if the man was as old as he had been led to believe, he was surely already in bed and fast asleep. But the old man's friend in America had been very specific about contacting him late at night for his own security.

Brian knocked on the door and waited. No one came. No light was switched on in the house. He knocked again a little louder and after a few moments heard a movement on the other side of the door. Still no light appeared.

'Pace Domnului.' Brian spoke this Christian greeting of peace in a soft voice with his mouth close to the door.

The key was turned and two bolts were pulled slowly back before the door opened just a crack. Brian again whispered the word 'Pace' and the door was opened a little wider to reveal the bent figure and worried face of an old man in striped flannelette pyjamas.

'The peace of the Lord be with you,' Brian said again in Romanian as the old man indicated that he should step inside the house. Once the door had been closed, the elderly man turned on a dim light and looked enquiringly at Brian. He still hadn't said a word. So Brian spoke to him in English and explained that he was bringing greetings from Richard in the United States. The old man inclined his head slightly in acknowledgment. The nod also informed Brian that he understood English, but still he did not speak. As Brian's eyes grew accustomed to the gloom he began to notice a few details in the little room. There was an old black stove in one corner and next to it was a low enamel sink with one tap, underneath which a large metal bucket had been placed. The tap dripped constantly like a Chinese torture. One wooden cupboard, painted white but chipped in places, stood up against the wall beside the table where Brian and the old man were sitting. But it was at the old man's face that Brian was now looking. It was very swollen and so badly bruised that one of his eyes was almost closed.

'What happened, dear brother? Did you fall?'

The man raised a weary, arthritic hand to his face before answering. And then in a tired, weak voice, told Brian the following story.

'During my Christian lifetime I have been in prison a number of times. As you may know, it was in prison where I first met Richard, whom you say has sent you to me. But two days ago I was released from the worst prison experience of my life, even though it was also the shortest of all my stays there.'

Brian waited patiently for the old man to slowly and carefully change his position before continuing his story.

'A few weeks ago the police came to my home and searched it very carefully. As you know, it will soon be time to celebrate the birth of our Saviour. My wife and my daughter had been very busy making Christmas cards to send to our friends. Each card was individually painted and beautifully hand-written with appropriate verses from the Bible. The policemen confiscated the cards and arrested all three of us. I am happy to say they did not keep my wife or my daughter very long but I was put in the cells and charged with translating Christian literature from English into Romanian and preaching during the past two and a half years without official permission from our communist government.

'During one of the interrogation sessions they brought a third, more serious charge against me. They accused me of having money in a bank in Switzerland.'

With a slight shaking of his head, he raised his arms in a gesture of despair and then went on.

'I admitted my "guilt" with regard to the first two charges, but declared my innocence of the third accusation. They became very angry and tried many tactics in their efforts to extract a "confession" from me. I was beaten many times, sometimes with the fists of the prison guards and sometimes with rubber hoses. My face will give you some idea of what the rest of my body looks like. I can only move very slowly, that was why it took me so long to open the door to you.'

It seemed harsh and tactless, but as the old man rested from the exertion of speaking and the distress of remembering, Brian asked him if he *did* have money in a bank in Switzerland. The question had to be asked because it is true that some East European believers *do* have funds held for them in the West. Their reason for doing this is twofold: first, they would not want to keep Western currency in their own land—it's against the law—and second, what would be the use of exchanging it for their own currency when there's hardly anything worth buying in the shops? They prefer to keep the gift deposited somewhere in the

West where it can gain interest, ready for the time when they need something specific which can be purchased in the West and taken in to them by a courier.

The old man raised his head and looked intently at Brian. He seemed to be weighing up whether or not he could trust this Englishman. It was obvious that this elderly gentleman considered Brian's question an insult.

'I have never travelled abroad. I have never met anyone from Switzerland. I have never received any Western money from anyone. I hope *you* believe me, the police interrogators at the prison did not. Their final torture was to make me stand in a concrete cell without heat or food for forty-eight hours. Every time my body would sag from fatigue, they would beat me to keep me on my feet. I was very tempted to "confess". I pleaded with God to send some angels to minister to me, but I felt no relief. I don't understand why He didn't grant me my request. I felt forgotten and alone. The only thing I can thank God for in that experience is that the torture was terminated before I yielded to temptation. I am an old man. I thought I would die there in prison. I *wanted* to die. But maybe God still has something left for me to do before I can go Home. But I am very weary. The fight has gone out of me. Do you blame me? Am I wrong to feel this way?'

Brian spoke quietly and gently to the old man across the table from him. 'You are many years my senior and our heavenly Father has given you a cross to bear that He has not asked me to carry, how could I accuse you or blame you? Only God can look into our hearts and see our motives. And I'm quite sure He understands your innermost thoughts and knows that you have not denied Him nor let Him down by agreeing to compromise. Even if you had, He would understand, still love you and forgive you.'

The old man nodded but made no further comment.

'Richard has sent you a gift. It is not in Western currency. I have exchanged his dollars into Romanian lei.

Those were his instructions. He sends this gift with his love and wants you to know that he will never forget you.'

As Brian was speaking he took an envelope containing the lei equivalent of $500.00 from his inside coat pocket and placed it on the table. The old man didn't touch the package. He didn't say anything, not even thank you. He just shook his head to indicate that he did not want the money.

'You must accept his love gift, sir. He would be very disappointed if you refused his help. God has been good to him in his adopted homeland and he wants to share His goodness with you.'

Brian rose to go. But before leaving, he went around the table, put his arm gently on the old man's shoulder and prayed for him, that he would know the peace of the Lord on his home and in his life, and that there would be no negative repercussions from this visit.

Before opening the door to let Brian out, the old man extinguished the light and whispered the one word *Pace*.

True to his promise, Petru was waiting in the shadows at the end of the street. He led Brian in silence along several roads to where he had parked his car. As they were driving back into the centre of the city to the no-star hotel where Brian was staying, Petru didn't ask any questions. Brian knew from previous talks with him that Petru preferred not to know anything about Brian's visits to other believers. 'What your left hand doesn't know, it cannot reveal when the police squeeze it tight,' he had said on one occasion. The only thing Brian said to Petru was that he wished he had known that the old man had just come out of prison. Petru made no comment.

Brian didn't see Petru for two days. But on that occasion he could tell that his Romanian friend was greatly distressed about something. When they were alone, Petru gave the explanation. Apparently, the old man had gone to Petru's home in a state of great distress. He was weeping and saying that the secret police had visited him in the guise of a foreigner the previous night and had left him a lot of money. He wanted to know what he should do. He didn't trust himself to make a decision on his own about this. He didn't want the money because it was a trick. Should he take it back to the police and tell them he could not be tempted to work with them for money?

Petru's face was full of consternation. Brian, too, was distressed to think that the old man had been so frightened. 'Thank God he came to you and not to anyone else,' Brian said. 'Surely you were able to reassure him that everything was okay?'

'No. I could not. It would not have been good for him to know that I knew of your visit to him. My left hand must keep secrets from my right hand. This is the way we have to work for the Lord in our country. If our dear elderly brother knew of my friendship with you and if he is ever interrogated again, who knows what they might do to him and who knows what his breaking-point is. Believe me, it is better this way. I prayed with him and told him I felt it would be alright to keep the money but, just in case he were ever questioned about it, he should keep a careful record of how he spends it. That seemed to help him to relax a little.'

Petru was convinced that he had acted in everyone's best interests. He could have quoted those scriptures I mentioned earlier, but he didn't. He was compassionate enough to understand the old man's fearfulness without being critical or judgmental, even though he himself is fearless in his work for the Lord.

9

THE INCORRIGIBLE
CHEERFUL GIVER

WHEN ANTONIN GAVE AWAY the new car we had
bought him three months previously, he didn't stop to
think that he might be putting our integrity in jeopardy.
We were well acquainted with this pastor and knew him to
be *generous, unselfish, patient, helpful, benevolent, humble,
honourable, reputable, kind, reasonable, honest, just, hospitable, gentle* and *fair*—in other words, *Christlike*—so we
weren't too surprised when he explained that another
pastor had been in greater need of transport than he.

'I knew God would supply my need again in His good
time, so I gave the keys and the car papers to this other
brother. He was *so* happy.' Antonin beamed with pleasure
as he spoke.

'I don't agree with you that this other man's needs were
greater than yours,' Brian told him tenderly. Then with a
little more intensity in his voice and a slight frown creasing
his forehead, he continued, 'You need a car too! And more
than that, *we* need you to have transport. You assist us
greatly by being our "postman" and delivering supplies
and financial gifts to families all over this country. We
could never get around to see all these people regularly
ourselves. It would take far too long.'

Antonin submitted meekly to Brian's pep talk, bowing

his head in acquiescence. 'You are right, dear Brian, but please don't be angry with me.'

I sat quietly through this little exchange, knowing that even though Brian was trying to be stern with him now, he admired this man's unselfish act. This was demonstrated as they hugged each other. Then holding Antonin at arm's length, Brian shook his head slowly and said, 'I despair of you. You'll never change, will you?' Their eyes met and both men laughed.

This wasn't the first time Antonin had given away things we had taken to him. In fact, we expected him to donate the money, the clothes, the food we regularly delivered. He received so much pleasure and satisfaction from assisting others in his church. But if ever it was our intention that something go specifically to Antonin and his family, we had to give it to his wife. She was more practical. However, never in our wildest dreams had we expected him to give away his new car.

When we left Antonin to drive home, Brian and I discussed possibilities for getting him another vehicle. We hadn't made any promises. After all, we had no funds for such a large project, but we had agreed to pray about the need.

'I hope Don and his congregation never hear what happened to their gift. They wouldn't understand. They don't know Antonin!' I said. I thought about our friend, Don, for a moment. He was the senior pastor of a large church in Ohio and had a great love for believers in Eastern Europe. He had arranged for a special designated offering to be taken in his church. The money had been used to purchase Antonin's car. 'But, who knows? Maybe there's another church somewhere, just waiting for the opportunity to be involved in a project such as this. But next time we give Antonin keys to a new car, please make sure he understands that he's not to make a habit of giving it to the next needy pastor who comes along.' I wagged my finger at Brian, indicating that he should be a little firmer with our well-meaning philanthropist.

It was late when we arrived home that night so we didn't bother to read the accumulated mail. It was fortunate for us that we didn't. We probably wouldn't have been able to sleep for excitement. Brian came bursting out of his office the next morning as I was washing up the breakfast dishes. He was brandishing a letter. Rarely have I seen him to excited. He usually keeps the 'stiff upper lip' reserved Englishman's composure.

'Read this! Read this! What a perfect example of "before they call, I will answer".'

I read the letter with mounting excitement. The pastor of another church in the United States was writing to ask if we had a specific project for a pastor in Eastern Europe. His church wanted to be involved in our ministry and desired to provide a one-time large gift as opposed to monthly donations. It was almost too good to be true. I could hardly believe what I was reading. The amount the pastor mentioned as the probable sum to be collected was almost exactly what was needed for a new car. In fact, it was a little more than necessary. But, as Brian said, the extra dollars would pay for one year's insurance coverage.

The only delay to Brian answering that letter immediately was a very sincere prayer of thanksgiving. An added bonus to us in this matter, although we didn't realise how significant this was going to be until much later, was the fact that Antonin was known to this pastor. He and his wife had made a trip to Eastern Europe and had met Antonin and his family.

As you can perhaps imagine, we waited impatiently to hear from that pastor again. The next two weeks went by incredibly slowly, but finally an envelope with the familiar return address in Arizona arrived. Attached to the short note from the pastor was a cheque for the promised amount. Things moved quickly then. Within two weeks of receiving the money, Antonin had his second new car in less than four months.

It wasn't until one year later that we heard the bad news. The Arizona pastor wrote us a cool, crisp letter. The gist of it was that he had been attending a pastors' conference in California. Pastors from all over the United States had attended. By chance(!), he had made the acquaintance of a pastor from Ohio, whose church had also purchased a car the previous year for a pastor named Antonin in Eastern Europe. He didn't actually accuse us of dishonesty, but he asked some very pointed questions. It was fortunate for us that this pastor had met Antonin. When Brian explained in great detail what had transpired with the first car, this man understood. More than that, he offered to telephone Don in Ohio and explain the situation to him.

How thankful we are that that man wrote to us. If he had decided not to write or ever to be involved in our ministry again, we would never have had the opportunity to tell him the truth. He would have been in bondage to ignorance and misconception; we would have lost our reputation for honesty in at least two American churches...and all because an East European pastor has a generous heart of gold. But God loves a cheerful giver, and so do we!

10

BORDER INCIDENTS

YEARS AGO I HEARD a preacher say, 'It's always something small that God uses in a big way.' As a young person
I abstractly imagined that since I was not very tall, God
would use me in some grand and glorious way! However,
since then, I have seen God use much smaller things than
little people in remarkable ways, especially at border
crossings into Eastern Europe.

There was the occasion when I led a team of girls to
Czechoslovakia. We successfully delivered financial support to nine young pastors and their families, ending our
trip in the capital city. Before returning to the West, we
took time to visit some of the tourist sights. Managing to
find a rare 'easy' parking spot in the city centre (by 'easy' I
mean diagonal not parallel parking; I'm hopeless when it
comes to reversing a car into a narrow space!), I took the
girls to see the old town hall and the astronomical clock.
The town hall is a beautiful fourteenth-century building
and the clock is incredible. We were just in time to see the
twelve apostles make their circular journey accompanied
by the bell-ringing skeleton. Then, taking the Jilska street
from the town square, we went to see the Gothic Beth-
lehem Chapel where John Hus preached from 1402 until
shortly before his execution in Constance.

On the way back to the car we passed through Wenceslas Square and took pictures of the National Museum, a lovely Neo-Renaissance building. In a preoccupied way I noticed there were a lot of road works going on in the streets ajoining the square, but it didn't consciously register with me that traffic in and out of the square was restricted. Once in the car, I confidently drove the route I knew like the back of my hand towards the motorway that would return us to Vienna. This took us through Wenceslas Square. Unfortunately, I didn't pay enough attention to the newly placed, moveable traffic signs. When I finally noticed the no-entry sign, it was too late. I was already in the middle of making a U-turn at the bottom of the square when a smartly dressed policeman stepped from behind a tree and blew his whistle for me to stop. There was no way I could get out of this one. I was at fault. I apologised profusely. I begged his forgiveness. I promised to be more careful in the future. He stood and listened with an amused smirk on his young face before writing me a traffic violation ticket. After I had paid the 100 kroun fine, he then politely gave me the directions I needed to get out of the city. I put the ticket in my passport and forgot about it.

About thirty minutes before reaching the border, we stopped on the side of the road, made a cup of coffee and held a little prayer meeting. We're usually more concerned with getting into a country than leaving it, but on this occasion we were bringing out some important tape recordings and it was imperative that they should not be found and confiscated at the border. They weren't hidden in a special place, they were just mixed in with our selection of music cassettes.

At the border we handed over our passports and money exchange slips and settled back to wait for the customs check. After about ten minutes three guards approached our car with grins on their faces. Handing the other girls

their passports one by one, the senior officer kept mine until last. I thought it strange that they were giving the passports back individually, especially since they had not yet made the customs check. Handing over the passports is usually the last thing to happen before the barrier is raised, allowing free exit from the country. Before giving me my passport, the guard asked me to get out of the car, then, instead of asking me to open up the boot for inspection, he ceremoniously handed me the traffic violation ticket with a slight bow and said, 'Don't lose your special souvenir from our country!' His colleagues were all laughing. I pretended to be embarrassed. He gave me back my passport and we were on our way. There had been no control of the vehicle. The tapes were safe.

You could never plan a replay of a situation like that. It just happens.

Unplanned Impropriety

Then there was the time that one of our teams was touring the southern countries of Europe. Macedonia and Serbia form a spiritually dark area and there are very few real believers there. In fact, until fairly recently, there was no complete copy of the whole Bible available in the language now spoken in Macedonia. We met a Methodist minister from that part of Yugoslavia who was actively engaged in translating the Bible into the modern Macedonian language. When asking us if we could financially assist him in this project, he used a sentence that fired our enthusiasm: 'Macedonia is in the Bible, but the Bible is not yet in Macedonia.' However, that's beside the point. Let me get back to the story!

All members of the team were very weary from the long, hot hours of dusty travel over unpaved roads. They had been visiting a few isolated believers who rely basically on the radio broadcasts from Trans World Radio for their fellowship and teaching because there are so few churches there. Everything is very primitive and superstition abounds. Before proceeding with the rest of their mission to Bulgaria and Romania, the team leader decided to give the others a treat by taking them into Greece for a couple of days' holiday where they could really be tourists and enjoy the sunshine rather than complaining about how hot it was. It worked! After taking it easy for two days, the team was in high spirits upon arrival at the border between Greece and Bulgaria. They were relaxed and rested.

When it came time for the customs check, the team leader opened the boot for the guards to make their inspection. The cargo of literature for Bulgaria and dental equipment for a Christian dentist in Romania was scientifically packed on the floor of the boot to conserve space. The guard wanted to see what was under the girls' dresses which were on coat-hangers lying on top of the luggage. One of the girls, a very shy girl, offered to lift up the clothes. Somehow, and don't ask me how she did it, as she lifted the clothes out of the boot, one of the thin metal coat-hangers became attached to the zip on the guard's trousers. She was almost hysterical with embarrassment. The man's colleagues were doubled up laughing. That was the end of the check! Who could have pre-planned that?!

Boldly British!

Another interesting border incident occurred when I took my mother on a quick, two-day trip to Czechoslovakia. It was her first and only time into Eastern Europe! The electrified fences, tall guard towers at intervals all along the border, the soldiers with machine guns walking menacingly around the car accompanied by their big, well-trained dogs excited her imagination and psyched her up for the 'worst'. I'm not sure what she anticipated the 'worst' to be, but no amount of assurance from me could convince her that this was 'normal'. She was sure they were waiting for us.

On that particular trip we were to deliver a slide projector and a complete set of Holy Land slides to a church not far from the border. I didn't want to tire my mother too much by making a longer trip with her. Crossing a border into a communist land can be quite stressful the first time you do it. The unknown makes you fearful. In fact, even when you know what to expect, there is still some tension attached to the event. So this was intended to be quite a leisurely journey once we were through the border.

After the usual formalities of currency exchange and filling out a special card for the vehicle, we waited. My mother wouldn't get out of the car even though I told her it might be a long wait and she ought to stretch her legs. Her questions mirrored her nervousness, 'Will they ask me any questions?' 'What will you do if they see the projector?' 'Will they speak English?' 'They won't want to look in my suitcase, will they? I don't want those men touching my underwear!' The longer we waited, the more unreasonable her comments and questions became.

After about thirty minutes, two guards approached our car. I had been silently praying that we wouldn't have too difficult a time getting into the country, if only for my mother's sake. I had also prayed that they wouldn't see the projector and slides, although, since we didn't have much other luggage in the car, I couldn't imagine how they could miss seeing them. And to be honest, I didn't know what I was going to say if they questioned me about the projector. I was relying on the Lord to keep His promise and give me the words to say if, and when, it became necessary. I opened the boot in anticipation of the inspection.

The man holding the passports asked, 'Do you have relatives or friends in our country?'

'I have many friends here. As you can see from the visas in my passport I come here regularly. You Czechs are very friendly people.' I was hoping my answer would please him and he would ask who my friends were. I would have mentioned hotel receptionists, shopkeepers, car-park attendants and others that I have become acquainted with over the years. But he didn't ask that question.

'Are you bringing gifts for your friends?'

'Yes.' I showed him the box of dehydrated and tinned foods, as well as the fresh fruit, hoping that that would satisfy his curiosity. It didn't!

'Anything else?'

'I have some baby clothes for my friend's new baby.'

He still wasn't satisfied and I was becoming a little anxious that he would keep on probing. He did! 'Do you have another present for someone?'

Without hesitation I heard myself saying, 'Yes. I have slides and a projector for a church.' I was surprised that I had volunteered that information but felt it was useless to try to hide them anyway. Of course, he wanted to see these things. For the next forty-five minutes I stood by the car holding the box of slides while this man and his colleague looked at each one individually. Occasionally they would make comments to each other when they saw something that interested them, but for the most part they viewed the pictures in silence. Finally he put the last slide in the box and asked if I had anything else to declare. I shook my head. Perhaps he didn't believe me because he went to one side of the car and his friend to the other. They opened the doors and began searching inside the car. My mother was asked to get out and had to stand helplessly by as one of the men opened her handbag and began systematically to go through its contents. The longer he took the more agitated she became. Finally, finding courage in her annoyance, she said in a loud voice to me, but for the men's benefit, 'Are they allowed to do that? I'm British! Tell them to leave my things alone.'

The guards couldn't help but hear her, and although all of my conversation with them had been in German, the way they looked at her and then grinned at each other showed they obviously understood English. I thought they would get irritated, but they didn't. Instead, my mother's indignant stance amused them. They put the things back in her bag and indicated that she could get into the car again. To me they said I would have to pay customs duty on the projector but they were almost apologetic about it.

Inside the customs hall the man who still held our passports asked me more questions. He wanted to know what the pastor planned to do with the slides. I was hesitant at first to answer but when he enquired if they would be shown publicly, explaining that he would like to see them on a screen and hear historical detail from the Holy Land, I felt comfortable in giving him the pastor's name and address so that he could make his own contact with the church. Realising that this man had the authority to confiscate the slides and the projector and to keep them for himself, I told him that the pastor was planning to give a series of illustrated lectures on the journeys and teachings of Jesus and that he would be most welcome to attend. After all, I reasoned with myself, there would be nothing secret about the church services anyway.

This man was most helpful to me after that. He took me to the cash desk, arranged for me to pay the minimum amount allowable, and when all the formalities had been taken care of he walked with me back to the car before handing over our passports and saying with a smile, 'Tell your mother I'm sorry she was offended. I was just doing my job!'

Although I had prayed that the slides and projector would not be seen, God had other ideas. I have to admit that I was a little apprehensive about telling the pastor that I had given his name and address at the border. It was something I'd never done before and I've never had to do it since. But when I told him what had happened, he was delighted, scolding me for not getting the man's name and address so that he could be *invited* to come to church to see the slides and hear the gospel. God's ways are definitely not always our ways, are they?

When Brian came back from one of his trips to Romania, he had an interesting border experience to relate. Although incidental to his real purpose in going to the country at that time, he also planned to deliver some new ballcocks for the toilets at a large church. This had been a request from the men in the church because these simple plumbing requisites had been unobtainable in Romania for months. During the border check, the customs official saw these things as soon as Brian pulled back the blanket covering the luggage. 'Oh, I need one of those,' the man said, helping himself and looking at Brian, almost daring him to complain. Taken by surprise, Brian was in the midst of trying to decide whether or not he should remonstrate with the man or turn a blind eye to this blatant theft, when the man gave him back his passport and indicated that the search was completed. Needless to say, Brian kept quiet!

Potato Salad and Pickles

On another trip to Czechoslovakia I inadvertently left my wallet, containing all my personal money and documents, lying on a chair at a pastor's house. At the conclusion of this final call in the country, I had taken out my wallet to write down the pastor's new telephone number. Then I had taken out the mission wallet to give him and his wife the financial support I had brought for them. I put the mission wallet back in my handbag but forgot all about my own. Not realising what I had done, imagine my surprise when I was greeted at the border with the words, 'Come into the office, you are wanted on the telephone.'

The guard's sombre tone sounded rather ominous but I followed him into the dimly lit room and waited for him to dial a number and speak a few words in his own language before handing the receiver to me. In those few minutes of walking to the building and waiting to be handed the phone my mind was doing all sorts of mental gymnastics trying to guess what was wrong. Had some unauthorised person obtained information concerning the important manuscript I was bringing out of the country to be printed in the West? I didn't think so. Who could have known which border I was planning to cross? I had only made the final decision on that point when I was actually on the way out of the country.

Nervously I took the telephone from the officer and waited to hear someone speak. The pastor's wife's voice was unmistakable. 'Gwynne, your wallet is safe with us. It contains your driving licence and some money. What shall I do with it?'

Oh, my! My mind was racing. I knew this phone call was being recorded and listened to by others so wanted to terminate the conversation as quickly as possible. The pastor's wife, on the other hand, continued talking. 'I called all the border crossings to Austria and asked them to look out for you.' The more she said, the worse I felt!

'Please, just keep my wallet at your house. I will come back soon to get it,' I said. That was going to be easier said than done, but I didn't know what else to say. She was satisfied, wished me a pleasant journey and put the phone down.

Now what would happen? The man sitting at the desk could see that I was a little upset. Almost apologetically he told me that I would have to pay 10 krouns for the phone call. I gave him the money from the mission wallet and accepted the receipt he handed me. He followed me to the car for the customs inspection. What next? Obviously he knew that I had been with Christians because he had the name, address and telephone number of the pastor on his desk. Would he be suspicious and give a thorough check? Would he ask any questions as to why I had been with that family? Would he want to know the names of other people I had visited? My mind was racing in so many different directions that I couldn't even formulate a prayer; I had to rely on the Holy Spirit to interpret my thoughts.

When I opened the boot, there, right at the front was a glass bowl containing home-made potato salad from another pastor's wife. This was her gift to Brian. In those years when he had been unable to travel to Czechoslovakia she had never failed to send him some of her special dishes as a consolation for not being allowed into the country. She still sent him gifts when I was the one to visit instead of him...in fact, she still does, even now! But the guard took one look at that salad and looked at me questioningly.

'Czech potato salad is the best in the world,' I said sincerely and enthusiastically. 'I dare not return home without taking some to my husband. I also had to buy some pickles from Znoimo,' I continued. 'There's nothing available in the West to compare with these,' I told him, holding up a huge jar of pickled gherkins.

He laughed, shrugged his shoulders and handed me back my passport, indicating that I was free to continue my journey.

Incidents like these continue to happen. Yes, it's remarkable how God can take 'little' things and use them to cause diversions and distractions at border crossings, thus keeping His hand of protection on cargoes and people.

11

'PRESIDENTIAL' VISIT

STAFF AND PATIENTS ALIKE, at least those patients who
were mobile on the surgical floor of clinic number 37 in
Poland, gave every appearance of commencing a rapid
spring cleaning operation—on themselves as well as in
their wards. Nurses were behaving like young schoolgirls
about to go out on their first date. They laughed and
giggled. They were borrowing each other's make-up and
doing each other's hair. The porter had been seen straight-
ening his tie. He was definitely walking taller with an air of
importance surrounding him as he moved slowly, because
of his arthritis, yet proudly, because of his position of self-
acclaimed authority, up and down the corridors. The
cleaning lady was receiving instructions from everyone
and constantly being told to hurry up with her work. The
women patients had all put on fresh nighties and the men
were impatient for someone to come and shave them. It
had been two days since any of them had had that luxury.

The only two people who were seemingly unaffected by
the frenzied activity were the quiet, sullen man sitting on
the hard wooden chair outside the small room next to the
staff room, and the foreign male patient inside the small
room.

'There's someone coming to see you later today. We

think it's the president of the United States.' Alex couldn't help laughing at the young nurse who was fussing around his bed. She had just put a long-stemmed, red carnation in a pickle jar on the window sill. The flower and the green label on the jar provided the only splash of colour in the whole room.

'What makes you think the president is coming to see me?' Alex was still laughing, not too hard—his injuries wouldn't permit it—but the twinkle in his eye betrayed his great amusement.

'The American embassy in Warsaw called our administrator about an hour ago and asked us to prepare you for a visit. Why would they have telephoned ahead unless someone important is coming?' The young nurse was very excited and just like everyone else on the second floor of clinic number 37, she believed the snowballing rumour.

Alex continued to smile and decided it would be futile to contradict her. What harm could it do to let her enjoy the flurry of activity, preparing for the 'president's' visit. He himself had no idea who might be coming to see him. Perhaps an embassy official coming to take a statement from him or hopefully coming to make arrangements for him to be moved closer to the capital city. He had been in this hospital close to the Russian border for just over two months. Since the collision one night between the car he was driving and a train, his only visitors had been a few courageous local Christians who were not afraid of the secret policeman outside his door, and curious fellow patients, anxious to look at an American.

I've reconstructed the story above from what Alex told us when we arrived at his bedside. I know we were a real let-down for all those people who had been waiting to catch a glimpse of the US president, but the little gifts we had brought with us were a consolation. For the nurses we had perfumes, the children received sweets and chocolates, the men were given ball-point pens and razors and

for the female patients we had small handbag-size mirrors and toiletries. The only thing Alex wanted to keep for himself was the toothpaste. His teeth hadn't had the benefit of a good clean since he landed in the hospital.

'We have lots of questions, Alex. Do you feel like talking about the accident?' Brian was eager to know the details and to find out if local believers had been involved.

Before answering, to caution us, Alex placed a finger to his lips and then turned on his transistor radio, positioning it close to a plug beside his bed. 'Let's have some background music while we talk. A man came a short while ago and worked on this "faulty" plug. So it should work very well now!'

Alex winked his eye. We all guessed that the electrician had installed a listening device in that plug. Hopefully, by placing the radio next to it, our conversation would not be heard.

'Brian, do you remember when we first met? You were giving an intensive training programme to a group of young people about to make their first trip into Eastern Europe. One of the things you emphasised was the very point I ignored and because of that I'm here today, all smashed up. I was overtired, but chose to carry on driving instead of finding a place to sleep. I was trying to save money and time.'

Alex was indeed 'all smashed up'. His right leg was in traction. Both arms were in plaster. He looked most uncomfortable. He couldn't do very much for himself at all but he didn't complain. Instead, he praised the Lord for this unexpected and unusual opportunity to have extended ministry behind the Iron Curtain. While we were with him, numerous people would come and stand in the doorway, just looking and listening. Alex explained to them that he couldn't talk to them just right now because we had come a long way to see him and we would only have a short time there. He promised to talk to them later. Reluctantly they left us alone. Apparently, Alex had been redeeming the time of his inactivity by telling his life story (testimony) to the people who came to his room. He would also read his New Testament aloud, sing hymns and answer questions. Communication was not simple or easy. Alex spoke some Russian because his parents had been born in Russia. And in Poland, as in all East Bloc countries, learning Russian is compulsory in the schools. So that was the language used in Alex's little room. But it was a foreign language for everyone. Understandably, he was very glad for an opportunity to speak English again.

Although our friend was in a private ward, the bars on the windows of his second-floor room, together with the man on duty in the corridor outside, gave the impression of solitary confinement rather than private care.

Brian questioned Alex about the local Christians. Had

there been any local nationals with him at the time of the accident?

'Yes, two Polish pastors were in the car. Though badly shaken, they were not seriously injured. They were directing me to the next contact place where literature could be stored while awaiting transporation to the Soviet Union.'

That raised two more important questions. What happened to the literature? Had the pastors been charged with receiving and transporting 'foreign propaganda', the name usually given to Christian literature?

'The literature and all contents of the vehicle, plus the vehicle itself, were impounded. But the car was so badly damaged that they released that soon after the accident when they had had time to thoroughly search it. I haven't seen the pastors themselves since the accident, but members of their congregation have visited me. One of them took a photograph of the car with the other one standing beside it to send to me.' Alex asked us to open the drawer in the little cupboard beside his bed. There was the black-and-white photo he was referring to. 'I am assuming from this that they wish to convey to me that I am still their friend, that they are physically well, but they feel it is better for them not to have contact with me again. I understand how they feel but I wish I could hug them and see them for myself.'

Alex and Brian were both silent for a little while. One of the things Brian always emphasises in his three-day training programme is the fact that in all our contacts with East European believers, their safety and their continued ministry must be our first consideration. We as Westerners can leave the country; they must remain there. I knew both men were now thinking about the possible repercussions these pastors could face.

Not wishing to diminish the seriousness of the situation, but at the same time not wanting Alex to get depressed about something over which he now had no control, I said, 'Why don't we relate some of our recent experiences to Alex? We had a very eventful trip coming to see you.'

The next hour was spent telling Alex about driving through a blizzard for several hundred miles with a broken windscreen; negotiating icy roads without a rear-view mirror or a wing mirror after both, within a short period of time, were unaccountably shattered; watching from our hotel window as a gang of youthful troublemakers tried to push our parked car down a snowy incline; the impossibility of convincing a drunken hotel receptionist that a toilet tank had come off the wall in the third-floor bathroom and water was pouring all over the floor; and finally, being commanded by an inebriated, hitch-hiking policeman to take him home. Definitely an eventful trip!

Our time with Alex went by too quickly but the fact that we had cared enough to make the long journey to see him meant a lot. He remained a while longer in that hospital but his medical treatment was not over even when he returned to the United States. In fact, there was a sense in which it had only just begun. X-rays showed that bones had been incorrectly set and that muscles, nerve endings and tendons had been damaged. Further operations and a lengthy rehabilitation period were in store for Alex. But to everyone who tried to sympathise with him, he would point out that what, in human terms was a tragedy, had resulted in many sick people in Poland hearing a personal testimony of Christ's love. He was able to say, 'mission accomplished' because the basic purpose of his travels behind the Iron Curtain had been to take the love of Christ, not only to take physical copies of the Word of God.

Training for Travellers

As I was writing the above story, the thought crossed my mind that maybe at some time in the future you might want to make a trip to Eastern Europe yourself. There's no reason why you shouldn't and, with the possible exception of the border crossings, you will probably find it a surprisingly friendly and unsinister place. A visit from you to a church (or to a family home if you have the name and address of a believer) can be an encouragement if you remember certain important instructions. Unfortunately, however, some people don't want to learn 'do's and don't's' from others with experience; they don't even want to hear them. They prefer to get on the bandwagon and do their own thing. If you're like that, you'll probably skip over these next couple of pages. But remember, there are dangers in paying attention only to Proverbs 3:5, 'Trust in the Lord with all thine heart; and lean not unto thine own understanding', without also acknowledging the truth of Proverbs 2:10–11: 'When wisdom entereth into thine heart and knowledge is pleasant to thy soul; discretion shall preserve thee, understanding shall keep thee.' The 'dangers' are not so much for the traveller as for those East European believers who are left behind to answer the questions and pick up the pieces.

It's important to keep in mind that each country in Eastern Europe differs from the others in the way communism is administered. And while one country may be applying a very hard line this month, it might have softened considerably by next month.

Hints for travellers:

1   It is unwise to take names and addresses of believers with you. They should be memorised. At one time we used to suggest that if people could not remember the foreign names and addresses they should write the person's name between the lines of a favourite passage of scripture in their own Bible and the address in some other passage. However, if border guards see even a personal Bible or New Testament, this sometimes triggers them to

thoroughly search the vehicle and luggage for other literature. So you might need to say like David, 'Thy word have I hid in my heart . . .' and leave your Bible at home. What's the use of having it in your hand if it's not in your heart anyway?

2   There are standard questions on visa application forms, no matter which country you visit. 'Purpose of journey' should be answered with 'tourism' unless you are travelling there to conduct business for your firm or as an exchange student with permission to study at a university. 'Destination within the country' should be answered by putting the name of a large town or city where you plan to be. *Never* answer this question by giving the name and address of a believer. If the form specifically asks for an address within the country, simply write 'camping' or 'hotel'.

3   When arriving at the border, you might find that any magazines, newspapers or books you have will be regarded as propaganda from the West and confiscated.

4   Keep your passport with you at all times except for the short time you have to give it up for registration in a hotel or campsite. This does not mean putting it in your hip pocket or shirt pocket where it can be 'lifted'. Your passport is your lifeline while you are away from home; to lose it is a very serious matter. And if you lose it in a communist country you may have difficulty convincing the local police of this. They've heard it too many times before. Ill-informed Westerners are often tricked into selling their passports to people who desperately want to get to the West. The gullible tourists are under the mistaken impression that all they need to do is wait a couple of days before going to report the 'loss' and all will be well. There are people in jail in Eastern Europe right now who fell for this con-line.

5   Don't be tempted to change money with individuals

on the street or in public buildings, however tempting their rate of exchange.

6   Photographers should take more than enough film with them. The well-known brand films, although usually available in the large cities, are very expensive. When you've finished a roll of film, seal it up in the box just as though it hadn't been used. Do this especially if you have taken pictures of believers.

7   When visiting believers, try to blend into their culture and customs. Men: don't stand or walk around with your hands in your pockets. In some places this is offensive. Ladies: in some countries it will be necessary for you to have your head covered in church. Ladies should also wear dresses or skirts about knee length and dresses or blouses with sleeves, or else a cardigan to cover the shoulders. And don't wear a lot of jewellery or make-up. In some East European countries Christian women do not wear trousers or shorts.

8   It's a good idea to have a supply of inexpensive ballpoint pens, chewing gum, razor blades, toiletries, perfumes etc., to leave in homes you might visit or to give to helpful people along the way.

9   Insist on a full explanation of everything that is not clear to you when dealing with officials in shops or offices. If something is questionable, check and double check. This applies to prices, schedules, times of departure, etc. *Beware!* Even if officials say they don't speak your language, they might!

10   When you're with believers, handle your Bible reverently. Never bend it or strike it. Don't put it behind your back.

11   Keep strictly away from politics in any conversation. Speak rather about your experience of the Lord. Do not refer to believers in the East as the persecuted or suffering church. Don't mention the Iron Curtain. Above all, remember that these people were getting on with the

job of reaching their own people for Christ before you arrived on the scene. Don't for a moment imagine that you have all the answers to solve their complex problems.

12 If you have an opportunity to speak in a meeting, (not legally allowed in some countries), but don't speak the local language, you'll have to speak through an interpreter... or interrupter, as some people say. To make it easier for the person interpreting, speak very distinctly, don't use colloquialisms or clichés, and use short, complete sentences so that the whole meaning of what you're saying is heard and understood.

13 Christians in Eastern Europe greet each other with a holy kiss, i.e. men kiss men and women kiss women. This may be a new experience for you, but it is a very precious and touching custom, not one to be taken lightly.

14 If you're invited into a home for a meal, be prepared to eat and drink everything that's set before you, asking no questions for conscience sake. However, the water in rural areas is better left untouched; it could upset your tummy very badly.

15 If possible, try to learn a few words of greeting in the local language, for instance, 'hello', 'please', 'thank you', 'God bless you'.

16 In communist countries, assume that telephones are tapped and that hotel rooms (and sometimes even restaurant tables) are bugged. Besides hidden microphones, some rooms have mirrors with one-way glass for observation of visitors.

The greatest peril of travelling in Eastern Europe is not recognising the dangers and not knowing your enemy. The real enemy is not the communist official, not poor road conditions, nor contaminated water. The real enemy is Satan.

PART TWO

12

INVASION

THE ROAD AHEAD WAS BLOCKED by four giant green tanks, each with a broad white stripe down the centre of its nose and back. As our car stopped, eight Russian soldiers slowly and deliberately surrounded us.

It was obvious that these men meant business. The way they positioned themselves around our car showed that they were serious about their special activities. The man standing next to my window had an ugly rugged face with an almost comical turned-up nose which he was rubbing irritably with his left hand. His other hand maintained a firm grip on his machine gun. None of the men were very tall and all were fairly slim. The one common denominator, however, was their untidy appearance. The only exception was the officer in charge who had shrewd, observant eyes, which darted from face to face. He was standing by the driver's window talking to Bill, our team leader. On the other side of the car were three other soldiers, one of whom was almost certainly from Mongolia. None of these others spoke. They just stared at us with a kind of penetrating look that was most disconcerting.

'What's the matter? What do they want?'

I was asking these questions, but didn't really expect or even want an answer from either my husband or Bill. The

weak noise that came from my throat was hardly recognis-
able as intelligent English because the panic that was rising
within me seemed to be squeezing my chest, making it
impossible to speak normally.

While Bill tried to communicate with the Russian
officer in a mixture of English, German, Czech and profuse sign language, I looked around warily at the dark,
unfriendly faces surrounding us. It was possible that these
men hadn't slept much during the three days since
the combined Red armies of Bulgaria, East Germany,
Hungary, Poland and the Soviet Union had invaded the
Czechoslovak Soviet Socialist Republic, but I couldn't
feel sorry for them.

Since our arrival in the country just twenty-four hours
before, we had become accustomed to seeing the Warsaw
Pact occupation forces in the larger towns and cities, but
out here in the deserted countryside, their presence was
even more sinister and intimidating. For one thing, the
loneliness of this straight narrow road held no comforting
signs of hope such as a house or another car. I saw nothing
in the present circumstances to encourage us. Verbal communication with these dirty, dishevelled boys was actively
discouraged by the way they prodded the air menacingly
with their long, clumsy-looking guns. Their dirty,
unpressed uniforms had buttons missing and their red
eyes could have been the result of tiredness or strong
drink; each chin was covered in stubbly growth and the
men had the appearance and mannerisms of desperate
criminals.

Bill and the officer were having great difficulty understanding each other and though I tried to tune in to their
conversation, the fear I felt made it hard to concentrate.
Looking back on that occasion now, I remember being
vaguely aware of comfort as I subconsciously admitted to
myself that this road-block had not taken God by surprise.
After all, He had clearly told us to come to Czechoslovakia

at this time and had, in fact, worked a miracle in getting us over the border from Germany. This thought brought an instant replay of the past few days to my mind.

So much had happened in the two days since we had heard the news of the Czech invasion on local Austrian radio. We had driven along West German highways to one of the smaller frontier posts with news broadcasters constantly reminding us that our mission was impossible. Whenever a sombre radio voice had announced that all border crossings to Czechoslovakia were closed, one of us in the car would tell the Lord that we were praising Him in advance for the miracle He was going to have to work if He wanted us to get into the country. We did not have valid visas. And what's more, all foreigners were fleeing the country rather than trying to get in.

It was more comforting now for me to reminisce over the last couple of days than to take part in the uncomfortable present. So I continued to remember.

When we arrived at the German check-point it was dark and the powerful white light of the arc lamps illuminated the whole area. No other car was in sight. In fact, the place seemed to be deserted except for the two guards who were hurriedly putting on their coats and caps in the customs shed. The lights were on in the office and we could see them clearly through the large windows as they came towards the door and out into the cool night air.

The man who approached us was getting on for fifty, with iron-grey hair cropped close to his head. He had a long, rather humorous face, and he looked very attractive when he smiled. I had the feeling that he wasn't taking us seriously, but then I suppose we were quite an unlikely group to be wanting entrance into an occupied country—a couple with a four-year-old girl plus another man. His voice was abrupt, but pleasant and rather deep in tone as

he asked us if we had heard the news about Czechoslovakia. Brian, who speaks fairly good German, assured
him that we were aware of the situation on the other side of
the border and it was because of what had happened that
we wanted to go into the land now.

With a shrug of his broad shoulders he stamped our
passports and walked in front of our car to raise the little
red-and-white barrier that was currently blocking our
entrance into the short strip of no-man's land separating
the two halves of Europe: East from West.

As we drove slowly ahead, he saluted politely and said,
'We'll welcome you back to Germany in just a few minutes!'

We didn't contradict verbally but smiled and waved,
being confident that God would open the way before us
even though it seemed an impossibility.

The contrast between the two check-points was most
striking. Whereas the German border had been brightly
lit, the Czech side was dismal, with just one naked light
bulb burning over the door into the customs shed. As our
car approached, however, a few more lights were turned
on and a tall, dark-haired man appeared in the doorway. It
was too dim to take in many details. The shadows were
deep and I felt an uncontrollable shudder begin at the base
of my spine and creep all over me. As the man approached
us he was buttoning the jacket of his light-brown uniform.
Obviously, he hadn't been expecting any business tonight
either! He saluted us smartly and addressed us first of all
in Czech. Brian answered him in German and the rest of
their short conversation was in that language. Out of his
lean brown face looked two of the saddest, rich brown eyes
I have ever seen. he stood about five feet ten or eleven
inches and was, I should imagine, a little over forty years
of age.

Brian held our passports out of the car window and

informed the man eagerly, 'We would like to get visas to visit your country.'

'I'm sorry, but that's impossible!'

Using a gentler tone, Brian continued, 'We've heard about the trouble in your lovely land and because we have many friends here we want to be with them at this time.'

Well, I thought those sad eyes would have to release the tears that had welled up under their lids, but with remarkable self-control the officer simply smiled, handed back our passports and said, 'I'm sorry.'

Surely the door couldn't be closed. God had told us to come, but this man, who was in control of this border crossing, said that we couldn't go any further.

Seeing our genuine disappointment, he leaned into the car and said softly, 'It's impossible tonight, but you can try again tomorrow morning.' With that he stepped back and indicated that we should turn around and drive back to Germany. It was obvious that our conversation had been terminated.

Back at the West German frontier, the guard simply raised the barrier for us to enter Germany again and gave another sympathetic shrug of his shoulders. He had been so certain that we would return quickly that he hadn't even bothered to go back inside his warm office.

Having no alternative but to take the whispered advice of the Czech guard, we began looking for a place to stay overnight so that we could present ourselves at the border again in the morning.

'Well,' Brian sounded weary and yet determined, 'our motto of many years is to be tested again: "Even if the door is closed, try it, to see if it is locked!" '

The village of Waidhaus was the nearest community and the Gasthaus Weisses Kreuz was the first lodging-place we came to. The small car-park to the left of the building was well filled and the hum of many earnest conversations reached us long before we entered the smoke-filled room. No one paid much attention to us after the initial glances in our direction. We looked around for someone to serve us, but the plump German Frau behind the bar ignored us completely until she saw Wendy, asleep now, in her Daddy's arms.

'Every room is occupied with people waiting for their relatives to come back from "druben"—over there—she explained, nodding her blonde head in the general direction of the border, as if to emphasise the impossibility of our request for rooms. However, after checking the room plan and talking in dialect with her husband for a few minutes, she informed us apologetically and yet with finality that the only possibility she could offer us was to share a room with an old man who was already asleep! It didn't take us long to decide that we'd better take advantage of this unusual solution before someone else with fewer moral scruples came along and took the last remaining beds in town.

As we followed the woman up two flights of creaking wooden stairs to our room, I couldn't help wondering what the old man would think when he woke up to find four strangers in his room the next morning.

Maybe it was because we were all rather excited in anticipation of the following day, or perhaps because the old man snored and wheezed in a rhythmic sort of way most of the night, that even Wendy could only sleep fitfully in the bed with me. In fact, it wasn't until the old man got up and left the room at five o'clock the next morning that we fell into a deep sleep.

Just one short hour later we took turns washing at the small low sink in a dark corner of the large room. Then after a rushed, but satisfying breakfast of fresh warm rolls, home-made apricot jam and hot, freshly-ground coffee, we got into the car. Brian drove to the edge of the village, which was really just a string of houses and farm buildings on both sides of the main road, with chickens and ducks

roaming freely from one house to the next. Just about a mile down the road we pulled into a small shady parking area to hold a little prayer meeting.

Believing that God prefers us to speak plainly and say exactly what we mean rather than to speak in generalities, we asked God to demonstrate Himself in a specific way. Brian's request was that we would be given permission to enter Czechoslovakia without undue delay; I asked God to keep His hand of protection on the cargo of literature in the boot of our car and Bill asked that we would be given guidance in the distribution of this precious 'bread'. Even Wendy sensed the gravity and earnestness of the situation because as we finished praying she sweetly asked the Lord Jesus to help us reach Uncle Ivan's house quickly and also to send His angels to travel with us so that we would be safe. So really, we made five specific requests. As we drove slowly on in silence I wondered what lay ahead. Would the door be locked or just closed? Would God open the door wide or would He allow a few obstacles to remain so that we would have to use our initiative and push the door a little bit ourselves?

At the West German frontier many people had gathered, standing around talking in small groups. They paid no attention to us but became quite animated as a red-and-white tourist bus drew up to the Czechoslovak side of the border. Several of those standing around had binoculars and began describing the activities that were taking place on the other side of the border.

It was a different German official who approached us now. His green uniform fitted him perfectly and accentuated his bright red hair and ruddy complexion. Without giving us a chance to say anything he informed us that it was futile for us to go any further. However, if we wanted to try our luck he couldn't prevent us.

It wasn't very far to the other end of no-man's land which, as I could now see in the brilliant sunshine of this warm August morning, had been cleared of all trees on both sides of the road. To the right, at periodic intervals along this ploughed strip of land, the tall watch-towers were clearly visible. It was the same the other side too.

As we slowly approached the red-and-white striped barrier in front of the drab yellow guardhouse, a smartly dressed Czech soldier saluted us and directed Brian to park behind a white Volkswagen with a West German number plate. After only a few moments another car drove into line behind us. This one was a blue Ford from Holland with a middle-aged man and woman sitting in the front seats.

As we turned around to look at the Dutch couple, Brian murmured very quietly, 'I wonder if Brother Andrew was able to get in yesterday?'

Andrew had phoned us from Holland just a couple of hours after the stunning news of the invasion had hit the

Western world. He told us that he already had a valid visa
in his passport and was preparing to leave immediately for
Prague with a full load of 'bread' so as to take advantage of
the confusion that would almost certainly be raging on the
borders as people fled before the Russian tanks. If all had
gone well for him, he should be in the country already and
we were to make contact with him in the capital city.

The 'Beetle' ahead of us was empty but very soon its
German owner emerged from the darkness of the customs
shed with the friendly guard who had been our confidant
the previous night. The duty guard here had obviously not
yet been changed. The driver walked abruptly to his car,
but just before he slammed the door and drove erratically
back to Germany we heard the climax of his verbal protest.

In a high, staccato voice, that didn't match his cool
immaculate appearance, the young man said, 'I've tried
four different border crossings in the last twenty-four
hours and although my visa is valid you still won't let me
in.' Then turning to look back at us he increased the
volume as he said, 'My whole career depends on my
getting in there. I'm the West German correspondent for
the Associated Press International and these people have
no right to refuse us coverage of this monumental news
bomb.'

For some reason the Czech guard ignored us and went
to speak with the occupants of the car behind us. I looked
at Brian but couldn't tell from his face whether his silence
was a result of quiet confidence or doubtful misgivings. As
for myself, I'd almost managed to convince myself that if
the press man couldn't get in with all his freedom of press
privileges and his valid visa, what chance did we have!
And then, as the Dutch people behind us turned around
and headed back in the opposite direction, my doubts
seemed well grounded.

When both cars had cleared the immediate border area,
our friend from the previous evening asked for our pass-

ports before walking smartly back into his office. Brian and Bill followed closely behind him. After only a short while they emerged from the drab building and stood smiling and speaking quietly to each other in the brilliant sunshine. Before I could stop her, Wendy had climbed out of the car to run to her Daddy. It was obvious even to her that God had worked a miracle and answered the first of our specific prayers—we were to be allowed into the country.

'We heard that Goliath has come to your country and we're on the side of David,' Bill said. For the second time in just a few hours I thought this man would cry. He made no comment to that remark but smiled in spite of his sadness. Obviously he had heard that Bible story and knew the significance of the remark.

Handing the passports back to each of us in turn, the officer said that we had been granted permission to stay in the land for four days. Wendy chattered excitedly to nobody in particular as we shook hands with our new friend and I asked the Lord to forgive me for my unbelief.

It wasn't until we were a few miles down the road that we suddenly realised God had answered not just one, but two of our specific prayers. Something had transpired back at that border that had never happened before: there had been no customs check of our vehicle!

The five-hour journey from the border to Prague was interrupted several times as soldiers stopped us to examine our passports and car papers. Although these men were very abrupt and wouldn't answer our attempts to communicate with them, invariably they would smile at Wendy, who was quite uninhibited in her exclamations of surprise at seeing guns and tanks all around us. These rough men never went so far as to answer her friendly wave as we drove away from them, but at least through these incidents I had seen them as human beings and I was glad that Wendy was not afraid of them.

It was mid-afternoon before we walked up the ninety-five steps to Ivan's apartment. Yes, Wendy's prayer requests were also answered positively. In response to our quiet knock, the door opened to reveal Ivan and his whole family in the entrance hall. After giving and receiving the customary Slavic hugs and kisses, we followed Ivan into the living-room where he offered a most moving prayer of thanksgiving in his delightful mixture of broken English and better German. He ended his prayer with these words: 'Heavenly Father, we have been unfaithful ministers until now. Thank thee for second chance to reach Russky brothers. We thank that you brought this great mission field to us.'

And now, as we sat in the car on this deserted stretch of road with these antagonistic soldiers surrounding us, I knew I couldn't honestly pray a prayer like that. I reflected on that reunion with Ivan and his family and I wondered how Wendy was getting on. She had stayed with 'auntie'. Ivan and his wife had insisted on it, saying, 'The soldiers are getting angry because the Czech people are opposing them. Wendy will be safer with us.' Ominous words, and now I understood their reasoning.

I was suddenly brought back to our present circumstances with a nasty jolt. The dark face of the soldier by my window became ugly and distorted, and all pleasant memories of the past few hours left my mind. The man beside me shouted something to his comrades and they moved quickly to his side. All of them became increasingly agitated about something. As they were all looking at me, it became painfully obvious that for some unknown reason I had attracted unwelcome attention. In spite of the warm August sunshine, my hands became wet and clammy. The wild stories we had heard in Prague flashed through my mind. People there said that soldiers were stealing watches, radios, jewellery and anything else, including

women, that happened to take their fancy. How thankful I
was that Wendy had stayed with the family in Prague.

As the soldier nearest the car reached through the open
window towards me all sorts of fears controlled my mind.
Would he make me get out of the car? Was he going to
steal something? I would gladly have given him a necklace
or something, but I wasn't wearing any jewellery that day.
My next thought really gave me some anxious moments
though: several Russian Bibles and New Testaments were
lying on the back seat next to me. They had been under a
raincoat. Had they been uncovered? I didn't dare look.
Did he know why we were in the country and what we
planned to do? Perhaps he was looking at the books, not at
me. I didn't move. Although I knew theoretically that I
should love these men for Jesus' sake, I couldn't help
feeling repulsed as the man's grimy hand with dirty long
fingernails brushed past my arm and tugged at the thing
that was provoking him. Earlier that morning, a young
man in Prague had given me a tiny Czech flag so that I
could demonstrate my solidarity with the Czech people.
Diagonally across the red, white and blue stripes was a
narrow strip of black silk, signifying the death of communism with a human face and Alexander Dubcek's experiment with liberalisation. I had pinned the little flag to my
dress but its silent protest was obviously too loud for these
coarse Russians.

When I handed him the offending object, he threw it
violently to the ground and spat contemptuously, grinding
it into the gutter with his filthy boot. Then, as the officer
handed our car papers and passports back to Bill, the
soldiers moved away from the front of our car and permission was given for us to proceed. Instead of rushing off
as quickly as possible, as I know I would have done, Bill
deliberately released the hand-brake slowly. He was actually hesitating. Then taking a small Russian New Testament from his shirt pocket, he beckoned to the officer in

charge of this small detachment of men. This erect disciplinarian strode over to the car and Bill motioned to him that he should accept the book as a gift from an American to a Russian. As the other men shuffled up behind him, the major's hard face became a little less stern, and his eyes lost some of their hardness as he shook Bill's hand. All of our specific prayer requests had been answered and we couldn't help praising the Lord aloud for His protection in this incident. It was a tremendous thrill to look back down the road and see that group of men crowded around a copy of God's Word. How we longed that their blind eyes would be opened to spiritual truths.

Apart from Brian's humorous observation that we should think twice before leaving Wendy behind again, the rest of the journey along deserted, badly paved country lanes was continued in silence. But I couldn't help wondering what else would happen before we could say 'mission accomplished'.

13

SUSPECTED OF SPYING

STANISLAV LIVED IN the old silver mining town of Kutna Hora where any evidence of former glory and wealth remained only in the unusual flute-shaped architecture of St Barbara's Cathedral. As we drove down the hill to park in the main square of this small town, the clocks began chiming twelve o'clock midday. Quite suddenly, as though a signal had been given, train whistles, car horns, church bells, in fact anything that would make noise did just that for three full minutes. All movement of people and traffic stopped during this noisy protest time. But then, just as suddenly as it had begun, the town became quiet as people moved into the town square, congregating in small groups.

Only an hour had passed since our encounter out in the countryside but that experience filtered out of our minds now as we prepared to make contact with Stan and his dark-haired wife, Lenka. Before walking to their home, though, our attention was captured by the pregnant silence all around us. The square was filled with people waiting for something to happen. Then the loudspeakers that had been erected on the beautiful old buildings surrounding this centuries-old-meeting-place began to splutter and crackle before the emotional voice of a radio announcer was heard. Everyone was listening intently. I became aware of a reverence, a dedicated attention, in fact, the whole square was filled with an almost worshipful atmosphere. Even the little children were whispering their comments to each other.

Bill indicated with his eyes and a nod of his head that we should begin making our way to Stan's house. He walked on ahead. I was a couple of steps behind Brian as we made our way slowly and thoughtfully over the uneven cobble-stones. Bill discreetly took one or two pictures of the tender, heartbreaking scenes as weeping people tried to console and comfort one another. But the expression of hopelessness and sadness on every face made it obvious that this glorious Slavic nation was in mourning. Their eight-month-old experiment with freedom had been murdered. Their 'Big Brother' from the East had quickly and skilfully stabbed them in the back.

After trying to identify with these anonymous people, we left the square and walked quickly, without speaking, past the untidy row of Russian soldiers standing outside the town hall to the area of town where Stan lived. We went along dusty, deserted streets where the houses didn't have the usual little flower gardens in front of them and where doors opened right on to the street.

'Lord, don't let anyone see us enter this home,' Brian whispered as we approached the familiar grey door.

Lenka usually kept her house door locked, but today it was standing open. Quickly we walked up the two well-worn stone steps and into the hallway, pulling the door closed behind us. Our friends were sitting by their little transistor radio in the sparsley furnished living-room when we entered. They embraced us warmly and tenderly but none of us could speak. Our attempts to sympathise were awkward and tears flowed freely as we prayed together. But although sadness did permeate the atmosphere, we didn't ever feel the utter hopelessness that had been so evident in the crowded square half a mile away.

Stan's brown eyes were bright with tears but his voice was steady as he began eagerly to recount some of the blessings they had been experiencing during the last few months. 'Our government has been telling us that we have freedom, so we have taken them at their word and have used this freedom to work for the Lord. We have held open-air meetings and have broadcast our services on to the street with loudspeakers. It has even been possible to advertise the times of our services in the local communist newspaper. Many wonderful ways have opened up to us for evangelism.'

'Do you anticipate that this situation will now change, Stan?' Brian asked.

'We shall continue to work until someone tells us to stop. They are busy now with the political problems facing our country. The only difference we have felt already is that we must have our church services earlier to enable our people to get home before curfew begins.' The excitement in his voice now became a little more subdued. 'We are not pessimistic, but realistic. We know that when the political problems have been resolved they will turn their attention to the religious questions. But while it is still day we will keep on working.'

During this discussion Brian unloaded the Bibles from our old black briefcase and Stan stacked them on the floor in one corner of the room. Bill then asked him if he would be prepared to accept a gift of money from believers in California, and to be responsible for its distribution to the poor and needy families in his church. We didn't want to take it for granted that this young man would be prepared to do this, but he assured us that he would be very careful with it and would keep a record of how the money was divided. As Stan carefully counted the money before putting it away in his bedroom, Lenka told us that lunch was ready.

'We don't have much to eat because many of our shops are closed but I have some soup and some cauliflower. It will be enough?'

Her last sentence was really a question and we all assured her that we were not hungry and she should not worry about small quantities. The vegetable soup was thick and creamy and the cauliflower was the most delicious I had ever tasted. Lenka's creativity and ingenuity had worked together to revolutionise this ordinary vegetable. Our compliments were genuinely sincere and she willingly told me how she had prepared the dish. While the menfolk continued their discussion in the living-room I followed Lenka into her tiny, inconvenient kitchen.

'You half cook (she meant parboil) the whole cauliflower in water and salt. Lift it out of the pan and cool for a while. Break it into little sprigs then dip them first of all into flour, then into beaten egg and milk and then into dry breadcrumbs. I then fried these pieces in hot oil for a few minutes, lifted them out of the pan and sprinkled salt over them. That was all.'

By the time the kitchen had been cleared of dirty dishes it was quite late in the afternoon and as we didn't know what awaited us on the return journey to Prague we began making preparations to leave. Stanislav insisted on walking with us to the car but conversation on the streets was kept to an absolute minimum. Only our quiet footsteps accompanied the chorus of radio broadcasters coming from every open window.

As we turned a corner into one of the main streets, we heard the Soviet's national anthem being played. Stan laughed out loud now and told us that this was the regular procedure when one of the clandestine radio transmitters was located by the Russians. These courageous broadcasters were keeping the Czech citizenry informed of the true situation in Prague because the Russians had already taken over the main radio stations. If, however, Russian soldiers were able to locate one of these 'pirate' stations, the Czech broadcasters would play a recording of the 'Red Star', thus causing the soldiers to stand to attention and enabling the broadcasters to escape. This sign was also an unmistakable message to the listeners that that particular broadcasting frequency was now off the air. Who could help but admire the ingenuity of these resourceful people?

When we entered the square close to where we had parked our car, we were surprised and then immediately alarmed to see a large crowd of excited people surrounding the vehicle.

'I don't know what this is all about Stan, but you keep in the background. We don't want you to get involved if there's going to be any trouble.' Bill's voice was firm as we hurried over to the scene.

Someone in the crowd recognised us and pushed us roughly towards the two uniformed Czech policemen who were taking notes and asking questions.

'Pass-a-port!' The gruff voice of the older man matched the stern look on his long face.

We tried to convince the crowd and the two officers that there must be some mistake, but since no one spoke German or English and we couldn't communicate in any of the Slavic languages, we were fighting a losing battle. After delaying as long as we dared, we had to hand over our documents to the younger man. He then left the group and walked to a nearby police car, where he passed the papers to a man sitting in the back seat of the orange-and-white car. As you can imagine, we were not happy with this development and our attempts to converse with the policeman became even more earnest. The people standing around kept up a steady stream of chatter and persisted in pointing accusing fingers at us.

Stanislav, meanwhile, was finding out from those on the

edge of the crowd that we were accused of spying for the Russians! On hearing this he pushed his way through the people, introduced himself to the officer in charge and offered his services as interpreter.

The noise died down and the people became less agitated as Stan began explaining to us what had happened. 'Someone noticed a Russian book on the back seat of your car. She has never seen or heard of a New Testament before and is interested only in the fact that it's a Russian book. Someone else remembers seeing you photograph the crowd. These people have put two and two together and are convinced that you are spies... Russian spies!'

We spent the next twenty uncomfortable minutes trying to convince the stony-faced policeman that we were not enemies of Czechoslovakia but that we loved his country very much. We smiled and tried to practise positive love on a very hostile crowd. After we had answered many questions, the people reluctantly began to accept our story. Brian fetched the New Testament from the car and explained that this was a holy book. In fact, Stanislav, who never misses an opportunity to witness for the Lord, preached a little sermon and read several verses from the Gospels. Finally, the people seemed convinced that we were telling the truth. The antagonism left their faces and the crowd began to disperse. After the policemen had shaken hands with all of us and apologised for the misunderstanding, they handed back our passports and drove away leaving us alone with Stan to pray and praise God for His protection. As we drove slowly out of the square many of the people who a short time before had been wagging their fingers in accusation now waved and smiled.

The journey back to Prague was uneventful and we arrived back at Ivan's apartment just in time for the evening meal. Wendy was full of excited chatter about her day with 'auntie' and only when she was asleep in the next room did we share our experiences of the day with the attentive family. As we took turns interrupting each other with small details of importance, Ivan and his family occasionally asked a few questions. Even though most of them spoke and understood English, we were inclined to speak too quickly for them now in our eagerness to relate everything just as it happened. Finally, as we told them of the little prayer and praise meeting we had had with Stan in front of our car, the serious expressions on all their faces relaxed and they began to smile. As we sat back, having concluded our story, they all began to speak to their father in Czech. We waited patiently for the explanation which we knew Ivan would give us.

'The Lord was indeed with you today,' he began. 'When our people become suspicious that a car is being used by those who sympathise with the invaders, that car is usually totally destroyed without any questions being asked.' As he spoke, one of Ivan's sons handed us a duplicated list of car number plates. 'This was delivered to our door today. These cars will all be destroyed by tomorrow.'

As the full impact of his words hit us, we looked around at the nodding heads and serious faces and realised that God was continuing to answer Wendy's prayer. The angel of the Lord had surely been camping round about us and had delivered us.

As we were making preparations to go to bed early, the quietness of the apartment was suddenly shattered by the noise of shooting in the street below. I ran towards the window but was pulled back immediately by Brian as Ivan turned out all the lights in the room.

'That's their way of saying "bedtime". The curfew is about to start.' Ivan's tender voice explained these things to me as a father would to his child. 'They are firing into the air and it is dangerous to stand close to the windows, dear Gwynne, in case a stray bullet should break the glass.'

From a safe distance now we watched as all the street

SUSPECTED OF SPYING   117

lights were extinguished and the tracer bullets carved up the night sky like fiery red darts.

Wendy and I slept really well and didn't wake up until the sun was high in the sky. Everyone else had eaten breakfast much earlier and we entered the kitchen just in time to hear Brian telling the amused family how he had been awakened in the middle of the night to hear running footsteps on the street below.

'I crept to the open window, hardly daring to look out and yet knowing that I would never get back to sleep unless I discovered what was happening outside,' he was saying. 'When I did force myself to look out I immediately wished I had stayed in bed because I saw that *this* building was surrounded by soldiers. I didn't know whether or not to wake everybody up but decided against that. However, I watched from behind the curtains as the men below moved in closer to the building.'

Ivan began to laugh and said, 'Did you think they were coming to get you?'

'Well, I couldn't think of another reason to bring them here. Don't they usually come in the middle of the night to take people away?' Brian asked.

'But, dear Brian, you are still here and the soldiers... where are they?' The twinkle in his eyes betrayed Ivan's amusement at Brian's concern. 'Do you have a guilty conscience?' he laughed.

'I don't know about that, Ivan, but I can tell you that I didn't get back to sleep again. I was waiting for the knock at the door.'

'But, dear brother, God has not given us the spirit of fear, but of love. We must show these dear boys that we love them. Let us go down town now. We have prepared some tracts which we will give out along the way.'

Sure enough, Maria was now standing in the hallway with an armful of leaflets. Somehow they had managed to get several hundred copies of the thirty-fifth Psalm duplicated and we were each given a stack to distribute in the streets. Even Wendy had a few. When we got outside, people immediately began coming to us asking for a copy of whatever we had to give away.

'Our people are reading anything they can get their hands on in an attempt to find the truth. We have it! And we may never get another opportunity like this to reach them.' Just as Ivan finished speaking, two boys on a noisy motor cycle rode up on to the pavement beside us and without even slowing down flung a folded newspaper to us before hurrying on their way.

'This is one of the many underground newspapers,' Ivan explained. 'All official newspapers are having to print what the Russians want us to know. But many secret presses are operating and the real truth about the situation in our country is still being printed.' Ivan read for a few moments and then began to smile. 'Brian, your soldiers last night were not searching for you after all, but for one of the secret radio transmitters. The building next to ours houses some government offices and they were searching there.'

On our way to the famous *Vaclavske namesti*, where the statue of good King Wenceslas on his horse looks out over the large square, we passed a very interesting sign which someone had written in white paint on a wall as a protest.

'KAIN A ABEL BYLI TAKE BRATRI', read Ivan slowly and deliberately. 'That is very interesting and is significant. It says, "Cain and Abel were also brothers." '

'So the Word of God has not been forgotten, even after twenty years of atheistic indoctrination,' Bill commented as he focussed his camera.

When we reached the top of the famous square we could see how people were shaking their fists at the soldiers sitting on the tanks which were parked underneath the trees on both sides of this long, wide boulevard. We

climbed up on to the steps of the National Museum to get some pictures of the crowded square with the majestic statue in front of us. Several military helicopters were flying overhead dropping leaflets. The people were grasping at the white pieces of paper as they fluttered down to earth, then burning them under the nose of the nearest Russian soldier. Obviously they weren't interested in reading Russian propaganda, but they had been eager to take our tracts or anything else being offered them to read. Our meagre supply of 'ammunition' had long since been exhausted though.

'I wonder if Brother Andrew was able to bring any tracts with him?' I looked at Brian and Bill as I spoke and saw immediately that we were in agreement on what we must do. 'Let's go and find him.'

14

MEETING UP WITH
BROTHER ANDREW

WHEN THE NEWS OF THE INVASION of Czechoslovakia was first broadcast on 21st August, Brother Andrew called our team to say he was on his way to Prague. I guess he knew we wouldn't be far behind him! And now we needed to find him to get more literature.

The family he was staying with lived close to the river. We walked steadily along the banks of the Moldau, crunching rolls of exposed film beneath our feet. Black celluloid was covering the paths, giving untidy evidence that the occupying forces were anxious to prevent publicity of any sort. We stopped for a moment to look back and admire the dignified silhouette of the Hradcany Castle. Below it rose the towers and domes of Prague—a city with centuries of culture and commerce.

The scene appeared tranquil and peaceful in spite of the turmoil going on in other parts of the city. As we stood beside the calm, smoothly flowing river, I could practically read the thoughts that were passing through Brian's mind. The sun was in the right position for a photograph of the castle from this angle, but I could imagine that he was weighing up the points in favour and against. Understandably, he didn't want to chance losing the whole film for the sake of one unnecessary shot. Just when it appeared that he was prepared to take the risk, Ivan rested his hand on Brian's arm. He didn't speak or even shake his head, but the way he slowly closed his eyes then opened them again had a restraining effect. We followed his gaze to the centre of the river and took a longer look at the man fishing. As his little boat rocked gently to and fro, we saw the glint of the sun on binoculars and realised that the harmless 'fish-erman' was in reality an armed soldier.

All of a sudden our thoughts were fragmented as a rapid burst of machine gun fire sounded just ahead of us. We joined the crowd of onlookers and saw a young man angrily refusing to open up his camera. The impatient soldier fired more warning shots into the air, bringing others of his comrades running from all directions. Their faces distorted with anger and excitement, these soldiers pushed people roughly out of the way and surrounded the young man, who by this time was showing signs of fear. In the face of such overwhelming opposition he had no choice but to hand over his camera and watch helplessly as his roll of film helped to make the black carpet even thicker. Truth had once again been erased.

Ivan walked on ahead and very soon left the riverside path. None of us were speaking now. The street that we turned into was dark by comparison to the river with the brightness of the sun's reflection on it. Crossing over the narrow street we followed Ivan into one of the tall build-ings and climbed three flights of grey stone steps. The dark coolness was refreshing. We didn't see or hear any-one else on the steps. Ivan rang one of the doorbells bringing a middle-aged lady with tidy grey hair and a clear complexion to the door.

'Dobry den!' The lilt of her cheery greeting was pleas-ant and the warm graciousness of her smile invited us in. In an instant, Brother Andrew and the lady's husband had joined us in the narrow entrance hall. In our enthusiasm we were all speaking at once, answering questions, asking questions, until the brother in whose home we now were said in a loud, heavily accented voice, 'We must first of all pray.'

His prayer, though spoken in a language we didn't understand, brought us close to God and closer to each other. Thoughts of guns and tanks, soldiers and politics, were erased from our minds and the situation was put back into perspective with God on His throne. Then while Ivan and the family moved into the kitchen, Andrew led us into the tidy, but over-furnished, lounge. The large room had a very high ceiling and two long windows. Wendy and I curled up together in one of the huge, over-stuffed, but very comfortable, armchairs and listened as Andrew quietly told how God had undertaken for him on the border four days earlier.

We then related our experiences and Bill added, 'We've never felt quite as strongly as you, Andrew, about bringing such large quantities of literature into this country because our first calling is to preach and sing the gospel. God has given us some wonderful opportunities for evangelism all over this land. We always bring as much literature with us as possible, but that's not our first calling. However, when we were in Wenceslas Square a little while ago and saw how eagerly the people were grasping after something to read, we wished that we could have brought in more tracts or small Bible portions on this trip. We only brought Bibles and New Testaments.'

I continued the conversation by asking Andrew a question that, on reflection, he must have thought quite silly. 'Do you have access to a literature supply that we can also tap?'

I hadn't finished speaking before Andrew was nodding his head and saying he could help us. He then added, 'One of my teams was sent to this country a few weeks ago to do a survey among believers. We wanted to find out from all the different denominations what the people here wanted and needed from us the most. In every place we heard the same thing, "Send in more teams like the Pioneers; they bring the Scriptures to us but they also minister to our spiritual needs from the Word." So don't apologise for having two strings to your bow.'

At this point Ivan entered the room, followed by the brother and sister. They set cups of hot lemon tea before us and told us about a large youth rally that was to be held at five o'clock that afternoon. Andrew was already booked to speak elsewhere so couldn't join us, but the rest of us made plans to be there. As we got up to leave, Andrew asked his host to tell Ivan where the supply of tracts was so that he could get as many as he could use. After that we said our goodbyes quietly with the customary holy kiss of blessing on each cheek. Until this point Wendy had been very still but now thrilled the family by calling out 'Na shledanou!' and waving vigorously from each landing as we descended the steps quickly.

The youth rally had been set for five o'clock to compensate for the 10.00 p.m. curfew. So we went back to Ivan's, picked up our car and drove in a leisurely way around the outskirts of the city to the Vokovice district, thinking that we had plenty of time. It was half past four when we entered the apartment block and began climbing more grey stone steps.

'I thought they said it was going to be a large youth rally,' I whispered, 'but these are apartments. It must be a house meeting.'

On the second landing Ivan followed a young man through a door. As we entered, several of the young people standing around smiled broadly as the wonderment and surprise at what we saw registered on our faces. We stood and surveyed the scene before us and were speechless. All the dividing walls had been knocked out and a large L-shaped room was packed with about 400 people. They were even sitting on the small platform which was situated at the one point in the room where the speaker could see everyone in both sections of the L. Every chair was already occupied and well dressed young men and women were standing on all sides. When Ivan introduced us to the pastor, Brian made some comment about his large youth group.

'Oh, don't be mistaken,' he urged us, 'not all of them are Christians. Some of them are here as a protest.' As we obviously didn't understand, he explained. 'Our government has been giving us much freedom recently but now we have been invaded by very keen atheists. These students have no weapons for armed resistance, so they make their protests in whatever way they can. Coming to church is one way.'

'Well, praise God! They're playing with dynamite,' Bill commented. 'The gospel is the power of God to blow a person to bits and make him a new creature.'

The meeting began on time with the pastor asking everyone to stand while he read a verse from one of the Psalms. The singing that followed was joyous and loud, and as all the windows were open, it was obvious that there was nothing secret about this gathering. Over in one corner there was a fairly large string orchestra of mandolins, guitars, violins and a double bass to keep the rhythm flowing. I glanced in that direction often because Wendy was sitting over there between two new 'aunties', holding her recently acquired 'singing' teddy bear, Big Ears. I remember thinking that I should have cautioned her not to wind up Big Ears during the meeting, but the next time I glanced in that direction I was horrified to see her doing something even worse. With a look of glee that was far from naïve, she leaned over to the instrument nearest to her, and by turning one of the pegs, loosened a string. Wendy's face was a picture of amusement but the look of horror on the boy's face who was playing the instrument was pathetic. As the singing continued I could see him leaning in close in an attempt to retune the string, but suspected that he was fighting a losing battle.

After several songs, all of which seemed to have seven or eight verses, the pastor announced an open prayer time. Immediately the young people launched into a flow of praise. As one person finished praying someone else continued. They were literally interrupting one another in their eagerness to pray, until after about fifteen minutes the pastor announced another hymn. When this was over he introduced us. Brian and I sang a couple of English songs and then attempted one in Czech. I couldn't tell from the smiling faces all around us whether they were happy that we cared enough to learn something in their language or whether they were amused at our poor pronunciation. Perhaps it was a mixture of both.

As we sat down and Bill began to speak, my thoughts wandered for a few moments. I remembered an amusing incident that had happened a few years previously when we had first begun to minister in German. The meeting had taken place in a caravan somewhere in Austria—a 'church on wheels' it was called. Bill had been preaching his heart out in German, trying to make the point that everyone is either a victim of sin or a victor through Christ. It was unfortunate for him and for all those listening that the German word for victor is so similar to the word for cigar. The perplexed congregation was being told that they were either victims or cigars! I wondered about similar verbal traps in the Czech language.

As Bill now stood beside the pastor, an expectant hush rippled to all corners of the building. His text was taken from the eighth chapter of John's Gospel in which Jesus tells the Jews that the truth would make them free. 'The Jews said they were not in bondage to anyone, they were Abraham's seed.' A pause then for the translation. 'But Jesus only needed to point towards the nearest Roman soldier to discredit that claim.'

As the pastor interpreted you could see everyone comparing that biblical incident with the situation in their own country now. Then in the middle of his sermon, Bill suddenly changed the tempo a little. He told us later that he had done this to regain the attention of a small group in one of the corners. 'I saw a notice down town this afternoon,' he began. 'It said, "the Russian Circus is again in Prague, please do not feed or annoy the animals." '

Response from the audience was immediate. When the laughter died down he continued, 'In the southern part of the United States where I come from, we have a little animal that could identify with the visiting circus. It also has a white stripe down its back.' Comparing the skunk to the Warsaw Pact vehicles brought spontaneous applause and relaxed the atmosphere. From that moment on he had their undivided attention and showed them that Christ is the only true Liberator.

In conclusion he said, 'It's never been easy to be a Christian. Jesus never promised anyone an easy time and it's quite possible that you will encounter difficulties if you follow Jesus and become His disciples. But if you want to follow Christ who is the Truth and who can make you truly free, then take a stand for Him now.'

There was a heavy silence as people weighed up the cost of living for Christ under a hostile government. Then after a few moments, young people began standing all over the building. This was their way of making a commitment. No 'heads bowed, eyes closed, no one looking around' type of appeal. More than fifty young people stood in full view of everyone to signify their determination to follow Jesus.

After praying for these young people and inviting them to meet him afterwards, the pastor opened the meeting for testimonies. Just as had happened during the prayer time, there was an eagerness to share experiences that was very refreshing. What was even more inspiring to us was the fact that each young person was expressing an up-to-date testimony of opportunities they had had to witness, either to the 'visitors', meaning the occupation forces, or to their disillusioned communist friends. The whole room was charged with expectant praise.

Then someone began to pray. Although I couldn't understand the whole prayer, two oft repeated words sounded unmistakably like Yugoslavia and Romania. Could these people be praying about the uncertain future of two other socialist countries that were currently experimenting with their own brands of liberalisation, I wondered? What if Russian tanks moved into the southern countries of Europe too. Would the Christians there be prepared for such an event?

The meeting ended at a quarter to nine and everyone left the building quickly so that they could be home in plenty of time before the curfew began. We also prepared to leave and as we were shaking hands with the pastor at the door, an elderly man approached us. I didn't remember seeing him in the meeting, but from the lovely expression on his face we knew instantly that he was a brother in the Lord. He gripped Brian's hand firmly and pushed a large object wrapped in newspaper under Brian's coat.

'Please take this to my brother in Yugoslavia. His church needs it,' was all he said.

Digging deep into a pocket of his long raincoat, the man then produced a scrappy piece of paper on which was written his brother's name and address. Brian promised to deliver the parcel as soon as possible and with that assurance the man left the building quickly. We did too.

When we reached Ivan's apartment, Brian took the newspaper wrappings off the parcel and revealed a beautiful leather-bound pulpit Bible in the Serbo-Croation language. As we touched it and admired the clear, large print, Bill looked across at Brian and said, 'I wonder if your thoughts are the same as mine.'

Knowing exactly what the two of them were thinking, I

said, 'Actually, as soon as those young people began praying for Romania and Yugoslavia I knew you would plan to visit those countries fairly soon.'

Isn't it interesting how the Lord can lead and direct your thoughts? We had never ever received scriptures in one communist country for delivery in another, so maybe the Lord was underlining the urgency of such a trip to us while we were still in Prague in order for us not to delay that trip too long when we returned home. I don't know. Anyway, with these thoughts in our minds we prayed for guidance and told God that we would trust Him to stop us if our thoughts were moving in the wrong direction.

The next morning we were up early. Our visas were about to expire so we had to leave the country quickly. Brian loaded our few things into the car to the tuneful accompaniment of the many birds twittering loudly in the tall poplar trees lining both sides of the streets.

Saying goodbye to Ivan and his family is always a prolonged affair with prayers, promises to return as soon as possible, hugs and kisses and so on. But on this particular morning the parting was even more painful because we didn't know whether we would be allowed to visit them like this again or if, perhaps, our next contact with them would have to be made secretly and under cover of darkness, as had been the case a few years earlier. When we finally got into the car and drove away, we could see the whole family—ten of them altogether—waving until we were out of sight.

About four hours later we arrived at one of the main border crossings between Czechoslovakia and Austria. On most of our previous visits we had used this border and had become quite familiar with the many guards stationed there. There were several other cars in line before us, forcing us to wait in the hot sun for quite a while before we could pull into the shade of the covered-in customs area. Wendy had just woken up. She was hot and miserable and

in the middle of my attempts to pacify her by offering
something cool to drink, a pleasant-mannered, soft-voiced
guard came to collect our passports. He recognised us
immediately and leaned inside the car to Wendy, touching
her hand gently.

'Wendy,' he whispered, emphasising the soft conti-
nental 'v' instead of the hard English 'w', 'don't be afraid.
We are Czechs not Russians. We are your friends.'

She managed a weak little smile as he turned to take the
passports into the office and, for a moment at least, she
began to take an interest in the familiar surroundings.

When our documents were returned about ten minutes
later, we drove underneath the red-and-white raised barrier, across no man's land, and back into Austria. A feeling
of relief, an indefinable easing of the tension came over us.
Catching our first glimpse of the grey-and-green uniforms
of the Austrian border guards was like taking a deep
breath of fresh mountain air. The strain of being constantly 'on guard' was now replaced with an informality
that was refreshing. We were back in the free world but
what about those we had left behind? The Lord had given
us many opportunities in the previous few days to fellowship with His people in their sufferings and we couldn't
disassociate ourselves from them even though we were
back in the West. We would remember those who were in
bonds, just as if we were bound with them.

It was late afternoon when we pulled into our driveway.
The next few days were spent doing the ordinary chores
that most people don't seem to associate with missionary
life. There were letters to answer, clothes to wash, news
broadcasts to monitor and a house to clean before we could
leave on our next trip.

During the week between our return from Czechoslovakia and the start of our trip to the south, speculation
was running high that Yugoslavia and Romania would be
the next targets of the Russians. After all, Romania had

refused to send troops to help in the invasion of Czechoslovakia and Yugoslavia had withdrawn from the Warsaw
Pact years before. People were saying that Russia would
probably put its whole eastern house in order. This served
to intensify our determination to take as much assistance
to our friends there as possible.

Loading the car with clothes, medicines, food and literature for our friends and a few necessities for ourselves we
began the journey south. Brian had the special Bible from
the old man in Prague in his suitcase. The rest of the
literature was stacked in various odd places around the
car. It had always been our policy never to deliberately
conceal or hide anything on our trips behind the Iron
Curtain, because we know ourselves well enough to realise
that if we did that, we would be inclined to trust in our
own cleverness rather than God's protection.

While driving up through the Wurzen Pass to the
border between Austria and Yugoslavia, right at the sum-
mit of a beautiful range of mountains, we were praying
that God would protect us and our cargo. But because
Yugoslavia opened her borders to tourism several years
ago we had fallen into the trap of regarding Yugoslav
border crossings as 'easy'. I think, on reflection, that our
prayer for protection was ritualistic rather than out of a
sense of need and God had to teach us a lesson that we still
haven't forgotten.

15

MODERN-DAY MIRACLE

THERE WERE TEN CARS ahead of us at the border. Normally this would have meant that we would be through in just a few minutes. But when the first car in line was still being searched half an hour later, we began to take a concerned interest in what was happening. For over two hours we had to watch as each car ahead of us was thoroughly searched and the occupants questioned. Our self-reliance had quickly vanished and our prayers were no longer ritualistic or formal.

The procedure appeared to be different with each vehicle. There was no set pattern to the searches. Some drivers had to take everything out of the boot and lay it beside their car ready for inspection; sometimes all occupants of the vehicles were made to get out while the interior of their vehicle was thoroughly searched—occasionally even the seats were removed. With one car the customs officials sent for mechanics to remove the door panels and hub caps, no doubt looking for smuggled goods. Of course, I knew if they found our Bibles and literature they wouldn't be happy but at least they wouldn't be able to accuse us of smuggling. That was the only comforting thought about this situation.

While we were waiting for the car ahead of us to move

on after the search of its luggage had been completed, I glanced across at Wendy. She was sleeping peacefully on the shelf behind the back seat. Her 'mattress' was made of Bibles and she was surrounded by a colourful assortment of toys.

Following the scriptural injunction to watch and pray, Brian saw two guards approaching us and said, 'Oh dear Lord, you know they won't have to look very far to find our precious cargo. We're in your hands now; may your will be done.'

Taking it for granted that our car would be subjected to the careful search the others had gone through, Brian held up our passports, switching off the engine and taking the key out of the ignition at the same time. However, the guard standing on the passenger side of the car said something to his colleague. Both of them bent down and looked inside the car. They were smiling at Wendy. Within a few seconds the man beside Brian handed him our passports, stepped back a pace and saluted smartly. We could hardly believe it. We were through and the check, if you could call it that, had lasted no longer than two minutes. There had been no thorough search, no questions, no need to get out of the car even. A miracle! As we drove steadily away from the customs area none of us spoke but I could see that Brian was keeping a close watch on his rear-view mirror. 'They've asked everyone in the Renault behind us to get out,' was his only comment before beginning to sing the Doxology.

I felt rather rebuked in my own heart and I think Brian and Bill did too because not one of us spoke again until we reached the first Yugoslav village, at the foot of the mountain. I had regarded Yugoslavia as an easy country to enter but the Lord seemed to be showing me that I must be careful. There's a fine line between expecting God to answer my prayers and taking Him for granted. I think I had been on the brink of taking it for granted that we would get into the country without any problems. So we had been allowed to see others having problems before God graciously made the way smooth for us. If they had seen just one Bible, a superficial search would quickly have revealed the other 299, possibly resulting in the abortion of the whole trip.

We drove on until we found an ideal spot for a picnic beside a shallow stream. While Bill studied the map, Brian and Wendy played in the water. I spread out a blanket under the shade of a gnarled old tree where we enjoyed tuna fish salad sandwiches, crisps, fresh fruit and a cool drink. It was a pleasant break.

By the time we pulled into the *Trg Republique* (Republican Square) in the centre of Zagreb it was early evening. As usual the square was packed with people but no one seemed to be hurrying anywhere. Older couples strolled arm in arm, some in deep and earnest conversation and others in silence; young couples sauntered along the pavements looking into shop windows, although there really wasn't much to catch the eye apart from their own reflection; and the student population stood around in noisy discussion groups. We had already decided to try locating the address that the old man in Prague had given us before doing anything else. So Brian wrote the street name down on a piece of paper and asked an elderly man if he could help us find it. Fortunately for us he spoke very good German and was able to give us clear, concise directions.

We drove to that area of town and parked the car a little way away from the address, then walked to the house carrying the Bible which was now wrapped in brown paper. We knocked on the door and waited, feeling very conspicuous. Silence. No one came to the door. We tried again, knocking a little louder this time. Presently a neighbour lady with straight black hair pulled tightly back from her thin face leaned through an open window on the opposite side of the narrow street and said something to us. We asked her if she spoke German or English. Obviously she didn't because she continued to chatter on in her own language. As no one had answered the door to us we assumed she was telling us that the family was not at home. Not wishing to cause any disturbance in this quiet street we thanked her with a smile and a mumbled 'Hvala lepo' (thank you very much) before walking quickly back to the car.

Our problem now was what to do with the Bible. Maybe you're wondering why we didn't leave it with the neighbour. Well, we've learned not to let your right hand know what your left hand is doing when making contacts in Eastern Europe. You never know who to trust or who may be an informer—even in the churches, and even more so with total strangers. So that wasn't an option. As I saw it, we had two choices: either we could keep the Bible with us and deliver it on our way back or we could leave it with someone we knew along the way and pick it up on our return journey. We all agreed it would be a pity to risk the Bible's discovery and confiscation at the Romanian border, so we decided to leave it with one of our friends in Belgrade the next day.

All the street lights were burning by this time, but the darkness had not resulted in a cooling off. It stayed hot and humid all night long. None of us slept very well so we got up early the next morning and continued our journey along the badly paved highway. Extreme care is needed on this dangerous stretch of road between Zagreb and the capital city. The scenery is dull and uninteresting and every driver's instinct tells him to hurry over those miles as quickly as possible. One of the biggest problems comes from the Moslem truck drivers who get out on the road, head their heavy vehicles in the right direction and go forth in the name of Allah! Honestly, that's what they do and they don't seem to exercise any caution at all. But that's not the only danger. We'd been on the road about an hour and I was trying to keep Wendy occupied when I noticed a farmer driving his horse and cart furiously through a field on our right. As we got closer he crossed the main road in front of us and continued his journey through the field on our left. He didn't slow down, he didn't look to the right or the left, he just drove his horse straight ahead. I suppose those farmers have been travelling those tracks for generations, at least for more years than the road has been in existence, and they feel that they should therefore have the right of way. I was just glad that we were travelling in the daytime and that Brian had slowed down in anticipation of what would happen.

Getting through the centre of Belgrade wasn't difficult. We parked the car and went to find the small wooden building in a back street where our friend lived. As we rounded the corner of his two-roomed dwelling, we saw the pastor standing in the doorway. It had been a long time since we had seen him and we wondered if he would recognise us, but as we greeted him his smile broadened and his tanned face shone.

'Gospod svama!' God be praised, he rejoiced. Then even before hugging us he asked, 'Are you here with auto?' When we answered him in the affirmative he said, 'God must have sent you as an answer to my prayers.' We looked at each other and waited for him to continue. 'I must preach in a village many miles from here tonight and I have no way to get there. Could you come with me?'

Brian didn't answer his question directly but said rather, 'Dear brother, if you are so sure that we are an answer to your prayer, then undoubtedly God will have worked out all the little details.' The pastor was beaming. Brian continued, 'We were just going to visit you very quickly before resuming our journey. I won't tell you in which direction we're heading, you tell us where you need to go.'

'Surely, surely,' his smile became a grin, 'the village is close to the Romanian border.'

Brian and Bill hugged him and laughed. This little incident was an encouragement to all of us. The pastor's prayer had been answered and we were assured that right now we were in the place where God wanted us to be. A good feeling!

Just at that moment the pastor's wife, whom we had not previously met, emerged from the darkness of their little kitchen carrying a large metal tray. She set it down on the rough wooden table in front of the small window before coming over to greet us. I couldn't help thinking what a beautiful dining-room they had...blue sky framed the picture, with a window-box of multi-coloured begonias adding extra colour and the shade of a flourishing apple tree giving depth and relief.

Mrs Drobni was a large, healthy-looking woman with her dark wavy brown hair partly covered by a little white scarf. Her rather faded blue dress, which reached almost to her ankles, was mostly covered by a darker blue apron. She motioned us to sit down while she unloaded the contents of the tray before us. The strawberry preserve was almost certainly home-made because no label decorated the dumpy green jar. Handing each of us a spoon she passed the jar to me. I was a little uncertain as to what was expected of me until Pastor Drobni explained this old Serbian custom of hospitality. I ate a spoonful of the thick syrupy fruit and passed the jar to Brian, who took some for himself and gave a little to Wendy. Bill followed suit before placing the jar back on the table. While this was happening my heart sank as I saw the pastor pouring a clear white liquid into small glasses for each of us. I had heard about Yugoslav slivowitz and felt quite sure that I was about to be given some. Sure enough, Pastor Drobni raised his glass and clearly expected us to do the same.

'May God bless you for coming at this time,' was his

toast. I didn't dare look at Brian because I was thinking of the time when we were in Hungary and all the men in that Baptist home had been given a little of something strong to drink before lunch. He had lived through that experience by turning to the open window and feeding one of the window-box plants. There was no way of escape this time though. We drained our glasses, eating and drinking everything set before us, asking no questions for conscience sake! We could not have refused the hospitality of these servants of God. They were giving us the best they had. And it didn't taste that bad either. It's amusing to look back on that incident now though, because the hospitality we had just accepted was nothing compared to what awaited us in the little village near the Romanian border!

16

FASCINATED BY FOREIGNERS

As WE DROVE ALONG the narrow country lanes, through countless little communities, each a copy of the previous one, the geese stretched their long necks and cackled madly at us whenever our car forced them to move over to the side of the road. And judging from the dark staring eyes of the locals, ours could quite easily have been the first car ever to have passed that way.

The two hours passed quickly as Pastor Drobni told us enthusiastically about his eight mission stations, where, because the older people had never learned the official Serbo-Croation language of Yugoslavia, he had to translate himself into three languages as he went along. When Brian asked him how he managed to travel to his eight churches, he simply smiled and said, 'Just as today, God always provides a way!' This intelligent man, who speaks nine languages fluently, knows the experience of becoming as a little child in his trust of our heavenly Father.

Presently we left the paved road and commenced an obstacle course across a bumpy stretch of ground. Unfortunately, the narrow but deep ruts which farm carts had dug out did not fit the wheel-span of our Opel. Consequently, we moved forward in a lopsided fashion. Children stopped their games and women ceased their conversations to watch our slow progress.

Obviously our arrival was causing a stir but Pastor Drobni seemed pleased with the excitement. 'The church will be filled tonight,' he smiled. 'Everyone will be curious to see the foreigners.'

The last house in the row of low whitewashed dwellings was surrounded by waving, jumping children. Our friend directed Brian to drive through the wide entrance separating this house from the previous one. As soon as we reached the seclusion of the inner courtyard someone closed the high wooden doors behind us. The family stood in line to welcome us. Last in line was the old grandmother. Her brown face was deeply wrinkled and she was dressed in black from the scarf covering her head to the flimsy shoes on her small feet. Two young children were hiding in the doorway, peeping at us and giggling when they thought we couldn't see them.

'This is a Romanian settlement,' the pastor exclaimed. 'The border has been moved backwards and forwards so many times, but that doesn't concern these people. They live from one day to another and most of them have never been outside this village. Everyone speaks Romanian. Only the children are made to speak the Yugoslav language in school.'

Chickens, geese, goats, cats and kittens roamed freely in the yard and a donkey looked lazily out of a stall in the far corner. Bits and pieces of primitive farm equipment were propped against the side of the house and the well stood in the middle of the yard, not more than thirty feet from what was obviously the outside toilet.

Before long Wendy and the other children were engrossed in a wonderful game of kitten-catching and it didn't seem to matter at all that they couldn't speak to each other. They were obviously communicating very well without words.

After a little while the grandmother called us to sit down at the rough table which grandfather and the pastor had carried outside. Spoons and forks lay in disarray and in the middle of the bare wood was a steaming pan next to a stack of brown earthenware bowls. Benches were brought from inside the house and the grandparents and other family members stood silently watching, waiting for us to begin our evening meal.

Realising that facial expressions can speak much louder than words, I was greatly relieved when the pastor began to pray and the staring eyes all around us closed, for any appetite I might have had was now gone. Even now—without any effort at all—I can see the glassy eyes of the old hen with her feet protruding like great claws from the other side of the pot. I think there were even a few feathers floating on top of the water.

I waited for the pastor to take the first helping and hoped fervently that he had a ravenous appetite. However, he simply spooned some of the water that the old bird had been boiled in into his dish. 'Very good soup to begin with,' he remarked enthusiastically.

All the time we were conscious of the gazing eyes of our hosts as we also covered the bottom of our dishes with the greasy brown liquid. Great hunks of stale black bread helped me get the hot fluid down. After struggling through the first course, I tried to say that I really wasn't very hungry, but Pastor Drobni had already started filling my bowl.

I sent up an SOS prayer, 'Oh, dear Lord, please help me!' These were the only words I could think of when I looked at the unappetising mixture of bones, stringy meat and flabby skin before me.

In an attempt to lessen the enormous quantity he had given me, I insisted on feeding Wendy from my bowl. I'm ashamed to say it, but my relief was very great as Wendy ate heartily, leaving me to nibble the dry bread. I couldn't

believe it! She was always so finicky with her food at home.

Towards the end of the meal the grandfather came back from one of the goats with a jug of body-temperature milk. Now, anyone who knows me *knows* I would never choose to drink milk. Even an ice-cold, strawberry-flavoured milk shake turns my stomach. But somehow I managed to swallow the half cup I poured for myself, knowing that the water from the well would have upset me even more than the milk. By this time, I was finding it awfully difficult to keep the fixed smile on my face.

This memorable meal was followed by good thick, sweet and strong Turkish coffee. The only problem being that the contents of the tiny cup didn't completely take the grease of the chicken and the sickly taste of the goat's milk out of my mouth.

As I helped carry the remains of the meal inside the

little house, I couldn't help quietly commenting to Brian that no amount of missionary training could ever have prepared me for the agony I'd just suffered. He laughed, planted a little kiss on my cheek and told me he was proud of me.

Pastor Drobni had been right. The little church was packed by the time we arrived. A few backless benches had been placed at the front of the otherwise bare room. All the old ladies sat together on one side of the room; their husbands sat on the other side of the narrow centre aisle. The younger children sat on the floor and everyone else stood. The small windows were all closed and the air inside the room was stale. As we entered the room the low hum of voices ceased and every face turned to watch us make slow progress to the front of the church. There was a pregnant silence as Pastor Drobni introduced us and about 100 faces stared at us unemotionally, waiting for us to do something. Our joyful music contrasted sharply to the rich, haunting, melodic minors of their hymns. Their voices had a certain coarse quality in them that could have resulted, perhaps, from calling in the cows every night.

When Brian began his testimony with the words, 'I bring you greetings from Christians in England', we noticed for the first time some audience reaction. It was an encouraging sign because up until then nothing we had done or said had brought any response. A little later in the programme, Bill mentioned that he had been with Christians in the United States and they had also sent their greetings to all believers in Eastern Europe. Again we noticed the reaction. It was not a sound, just a sensation that passed around the room.

The service lasted two and a half hours. As we walked back along the street to the last house, we questioned Pastor Drobni about this reaction of the people to our greetings from other Christians. 'You must try to understand,' he patiently told us, 'no one has ever visited these people before. You are the first Christians from abroad to come to this village. Your being here has underlined something I have been trying to tell them for years, and that is, that God has His people all over the world, but as they'd never met any other Christians they couldn't grasp it.' I made the comment that that would account for their silence and stares.

'Yes, please, dear Gwynne, dear Brian, dear Bill, do not be upset by their faces. You were like angels from heaven to them.'

By this time we were all inside the little kitchen. As we weren't quite sure what was expected of us now, I asked if the family had a Bible. The pastor said something to the grandmother who went to a cupboard and carefully lifted a very old and tattered Bible on to the table. She handled it with extreme care, bordering on devotion, and I was ashamed of the way I had just carelessly pushed Brian's Bible across the table towards him.

After reading a Psalm together, grandfather prayed. We were then shown into the bedroom which was furnished with one very large bed and a heavy dark wardrobe. The door was closed behind us and Brian and I looked questioningly at each other. Were we all—Bill as well—to sleep in this one room, in this one bed? The answer was obvious. Yes!

Wendy found this situation very amusing and laughed with delight. But we were sobered by the fact that these other people and the pastor must be sleeping on the earthen floor in the kitchen next door because that was the only other room in the house. What love these people were showing us. They had gladly given the best they could offer—their family bed. As we pondered on this act of hospitality, the unusualness of the situation and the 'aroma' from the bed sheets (which obviously hadn't been changed for quite a while!) faded into insignificance.

During a breakfast of black bread, tomatoes, goat's

cheese and home-made sausage, we asked the pastor if we should leave some Bibles here. He paused for a moment before answering. 'There are only a few old Bibles in this village, but over the border in Romania you will find whole churches without a complete copy of the Word of God. Some pastors don't even have a Bible of their own. Take what you have and give to them.'

After holy kisses, handshakes and hugs all round, we drove towards the Romanian border pondering Pastor Drobni's words. It wasn't until we were a few miles down the road that we began to wonder how he would get back to Belgrade. But instinctively we knew that the Lord would provide a way for him.

We never got to know the names of those people, but we'll never forget them. And with that taste of Romanian hospitality, I couldn't help wondering what awaited us over the border!

17

OUR SECRET WEAPON

THE LITTLE RED-AND-WHITE shield was warning us that the Romanian border was only 1,500 metres away.

'We're close to the crossing-point,' Bill said, 'let's pull over and pray.'

The next fifteen minutes were spent reminding God that He'd brought us this far and asking Him for His help to get over the border without hindrance. Then, before moving on, Bill and Brian made a check of the car to see if the load had become dislodged in any place. As they were making some minor readjustments they saw the Bible! We had forgotten to leave it with Pastor Drobni. And that had been our prime reason for visiting him in Belgrade. Now what were we going to do?

'There's no alternative,' Bill said, 'we'll have to take it with us and hope they don't see it at the border.'

None of us felt really happy about this. It was such a big book and the Romanians were notorious for their thorough searches of vehicles entering their country from abroad. But after another, very specific, prayer, we drove on. All this time Wendy was enjoying her mid-morning nap.

Just a few minutes later we came in sight of the border. A large poster welcomed us to the Glorious Peoples'

Republic of Romania and a friendly young guard pointed to where we should park. He took the passports and car papers and sauntered casually back into the low office building.

'This doesn't look too favourable,' mentioned Brian. 'There's only one other car here, so they have plenty of time to make a thorough search if they want to.'

Our situation looked even bleaker when two armed guards approached the other car and asked the driver to take everything out of the boot. I wondered if they had a specific reason for doing this, because when that search revealed nothing out of the ordinary, they asked the driver, who was a small, stocky man, to take off the hub caps from all four wheels.

By this time Bill and Brian had gone into the office in an attempt to accelerate the red tape bureaucracy, hoping that in so doing our search would be less intense because they still had the other car to inspect. That was human reasoning, not God's solution.

Wendy woke up just as mechanics were removing the door panels of the other car. This procedure interested her, so she clambered out of the car to get a closer look. I was afraid that any movement would attract unwanted attention in our direction, so sat still and prayed that God would blind the eyes of the guards to our literature. Now that Wendy had left her bed, they would only have to lift the blanket to see a large part of our cargo. I wondered whether to straighten the cover or to leave it rumpled. Which would look more natural? I decided to leave it. At about the same time, Bill and Brian opened the glass door and came out of the building with two guards. I noticed that one of the officers was still holding our passports. Now would come the search.

When Wendy noticed Brian, she ran to her Daddy shouting, 'Daddy, Daddy, come quickly and see what they're doing to this poor man's car.' Her eyes were big with wonder and her voice was urgent with incredulity. The way she pointed and tugged at her Daddy to go and have a look seemed to amuse the guards who were just standing looking at her. Then, as so often happens with small children, she forgot for a few minutes her interest in the other car and remembered her tummy.

'Mummy, may I please have some fudge?' Almost before I could say 'yes', she had dived for the blue bag at my feet in her search for the chocolate fudge I had made prior to the journey. Then something happened that was completely unrehearsed but which the Lord used to get us through the border quickly. Wendy remembered her manners and began offering fudge to her Daddy, to Uncle Bill and on down the line to the two guards. Bill had just opened the boot lid for the inspection when this happened and the two men became so occupied with the polite little blonde-haired child that they seemed to completely forget their purpose for being there. The one man handed our passports back to Brian as he bent down to Wendy's level and tried to speak to her in English. The other man took a quick glance in the boot but didn't touch anything or ask to see inside any of the suitcases. With many smiles, waves and best wishes for a pleasant stay in their land, they lifted the barrier and let us through. The big, black Croation Bible was safe! The Romanian literature was also safe!

'They would have been suspicious if any one of us had offered them fudge, but from our little secret weapon it was the perfect foil,' Bill rejoiced.

Premier Nicolai Ceaucescu had not sent any Romanian troops to join the other Warsaw Pact countries in their invasion of Czechoslovakia and it seemed that the Russians, Poles, East Germans, Hungarians and Bulgarians were upset with him over this. Those countries with common borders mobilised their troops along the Romanian frontiers. In response to this, Ceaucescu had ordered a full mobilisation of Romanian forces just prior to our arrival in the country. This meant that office and factory workers alike had received rifles and automatic weapons; every student between the ages of eighteen and twenty-one was receiving military instruction several days a week. People all over the country were fearful of a Czech-type invasion.

However, we found excitement within the circles of believers. Because the police were preoccupied with the anticipated invasion, believers everywhere were becoming bolder and more courageous in their witness. We travelled the length and breadth of the country visiting families in large towns as well as the small villages, and in almost every family we met there was someone who had been in prison for their Christian faith.

In one small suburban home we met with almost 100 believers. Every room in that little house was filled with people. They were sitting on furniture, including the beds, on every available inch of floor space and standing all around the walls. It was here that I made a very big mistake. The meeting lasted several hours, until, under cover of darkness, the people were reluctantly leaving in small groups of twos and threes so as not to attract the attention of informers in the area. Although why they bothered I'll never know. No one could have missed seeing so many people enter that home in the early evening or failed to hear the singing of so many rich voices. Anyway, we were standing near the door, hugging the people as they left, when one young man quietly asked me if we had any Bibles. Without thinking, I answered truthfully. A ripple of anticipation spread throughout the room and since we were eager to place our literature in the hands of believers who would use it, I saw no reason why we shouldn't let these people have our remaining stock. Brian and Bill were in agreement, so we took our leave of the church leaders and walked to our car which was parked about a mile away.

A few of the young people followed us at a distance.

However, word had spread among those still in the home that we had Bibles in our car and by the time we arrived at our vehicle about thirty people had joined us, all with outstretched hands, hoping for a Bible. The friend who had taken us to the meeting became very agitated and insisted that we drive away and leave those people empty-handed. I didn't understand this at all and asked for an explanation.

'Gwynne, it is very dangerous for us and for them. We must leave at once.' Mihai was already in the car and urging us to drive away.

Once we were on the road he assured us that our Bibles would reach those people, but it had to be done quietly and slowly—not the big hand-out we had been planning. What a disappointment! And I was embarrassed that my ignorance of the local situation had caused Mihai to be upset.

As we said goodbye to him outside his home several miles away, he once again assured us that he would deliver the Bibles to the people we had just left. It was very late and the streets were deserted, so he was able to carry our remaining cargo of literature to his flat without arousing the suspicion of nosey neighbours.

'The only Bible in our possession now is the pulpit Bible for the church in Yugoslavia. Tomorrow or the next day we'll try to deliver that,' Bill said as we pulled up and parked outside the dismal hotel we were staying in.

It was raining hard the next morning, so Brian didn't spend a lot of time trying to conceal the Bible. In fact, he simply placed it on the right-hand side of the boot underneath a towel so that it would not be damaged by the suitcases.

'I'll put it here because the customs check is usually made from the left-hand side of the car. Hopefully they won't see it,' he said to Bill, closing the lid and jumping into the car.

Two hours later we approached the border area. Once again we asked for God's protection on the Bible, asking Him to 'blind' the guards' eyes to its presence. God didn't answer that prayer, at least, not the second part of the prayer. The customs officials saluted as they approached the car and indicated that someone should unlock the boot for inspection. Brian got out and stood on the right-hand side of the car, hoping to block the men's access to that side of the boot. It didn't work. The tall, younger man reached across the suitcases, put his hand down the side and pulled out the Bible. It was just as if he had been standing at the car watching Brian place the Bible that morning. Now what would happen? He tore open the wrapping paper and opened the book roughly, frowned and said something to the senior officer who had been silently watching all this. The older man took the Bible gently from him, closed it and said simply, 'Biblia', with a kind of reverence in his voice. There were no questions, no accusations, no difficult moments. He handed the Bible back to Brian with a smile, shook hands very enthusiastically, saluted and handed our passports back, indicating that the customs check was over and we were free to travel on. Someone in Romania had told us on one of our previous trips that there was a believer on one of the border posts. I think we met him that day!

Delivering the Bible to the church in Yugoslavia went like clockwork and each one of us was thankful that we had been hindered from delivering it on our outward journey. Lesson learned? God's timing is always perfect!

SPOTLIGHT FOR PRAYER

I would like to ask you to pray for all those I've mentioned in this book. Even though I've sometimes had to use assumed names for believers in the East, God knows their identity. Others have remained anonymous; even so, God knows the ones referred to.

I would also like to draw your attention to the fact that a ministry in Eastern Europe requires not only those who are called and prepared to be on the front line of battle in a travelling ministry, but also those, like yourselves, who are prepared to remain at home, praying and supporting those in the combat area. The statistics on the following pages will assist you to focus on topics for prayer.

In 1 Samuel 30:24 David sets forth the principle that both groups—those at home and those who go—must share equally in the spoils of battle. So whether it be you at home, or those of us who travel behind enemy lines into Eastern Europe, we are all essential to the overall ministry and all must share in the rewards and spiritual dividends. I've written these stories so that you, too, can rejoice over the victories won on the battlefield of Eastern Europe.

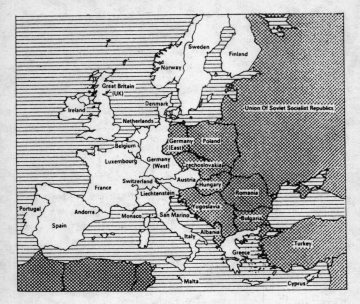

BULGARIA

The people are mainly Slav and have close ethnic and linguistic ties with Russia. Bulgaria is often described as the bridge between the Middle East and Europe. It is regularly crossed by motorists and heavy transport on the way from Western Europe through Yugoslavia to Istanbul in Turkey. Street names and road signs are in the Cyrillic script but also in Roman letters on the main highways.

The country is renowned for its yoghurt, a staple part of the diet, which is thought to be the main contribution to the longevity of the people. National dishes include guvech, *pieces of meat and assorted vegetables;* sarmi, *stuffed cabbage rolls with vine leaves; and* shishceta, *pieces of spiced lamb on a skewer.*

Area 110,900 sq. km. One of the Balkan states.
Population 8,900,000. Annual growth 0.2%. People per sq. km. 80.

Peoples
Bulgarian 83%. A Slavic people.
Turk 8.5%. Turkey was the ruling power for 500 years.
Other minorities 8.5%. Gypsy 460,000; Macedonian 231,000; Armenian 30,000; Russian 25,000; Gagauz 16,000; Jew 7,000; Greek 7,000; Tatar 5,500.
Literacy 98%. Official language: Bulgarian (Slavic). All languages 9. Bible translations 3Bi 1NT 4por.
Capital: Sofia 1,200,000. Urbanization 60%.
Economy: Rapid industrialization and favourable trade agreements with USSR and less centralization of the economy have brought improvements in standards of living.
Politics: Independent from Turkey in 1878. Communist rule since 1944. A hard line Marxist regime that is faithful to the USSR. Bulgaria is sometimes called 'Little Russia'.
Religion: Severe limitation and control of all organized religious groups. Church leaders are often government appointees.
Non-religious/Atheist: 25.3%.
Muslim 10.4%. Turk 30% of Gypsies, Pomak (Bulgar Muslims 300,000). Tatar.
Christian 64.2%.
Bulgarian Orthodox 61.7%. Practising 20%. 5,500,000a; 4,220,000m. The chief preserver of the national culture during the centuries of Turkish rule. Heavily infiltrated by Marxists.
Roman Catholic 0.7%. 66,000a; 51,000m. Severely persecuted at times.
Armenian Orthodox 0.25%.
Protestant 0.58%. 51,600a, 33,000m. Denominations 10. Largest (adult members):

Pentecostal Church	14,000
Congregational Church	4,700
Brethren Assemblies	est. 3,800
Seventh Day Adventist Church	3,400
Methodist Church	1,150
Baptist Church	720

Evangelical 0.54% of population.
Missionaries to Bulgaria 0.

CZECHOSLOVAKIA

Czechoslovakia is situated in the heart of Europe. The country is full of monuments from its medieval past and is renowned for its natural beauty, its music and its architecture.

The capital, Prague, lies among pleasant hills on the River

Vltava. Prague was a great city even in the Middle Ages and dating from this time are some fine buildings such as Prague Castle—the Hradcany, and the Charles University, founded by Charles IV in 1348, the oldest in Central Europe. Prague is also the city of Jan (John) Hus, the 15th century preacher whose reforming ideas pre-dated Luther.

The local food is tasty and very filling. Pork is the most popular meat and is often served with dumplings. In fact, roast pork, well done and served with sauerkraut and dumplings has become a national dish.

Area 128,000 sq. km. Landlocked state in central Europe.

Population 15,500,000. Annual growth 0.3%. People per sq.km. 121.

Peoples

Czech 62.5%. In centre and west.

Slovak 29%. In east.

Other minorities 8.5%. Magyar (Hungarian) 620,000; Gypsy 385,000; Polish 80,000; German 77,000.

USSR forces, etc. 110,000.

Literacy 99%. Official languages: Czech, Slovak.

All languages 8. Bible translations 6Bi 1por.

Capital: Prague 1,300,000. Urbanization 74%.

Economy: Highly industrialized and efficient before the Communist takeover. Now economy tied to that of Russia by disadvantageous trade agreements.

Politics: A federal republic of two nations—Czechs (Bohemia, Moravia and parts of Silesia) in the west and Slovaks in the east. Although a minority party, the Communists seized power in 1948. The liberalizing policies of the Dubcek Government (1966–68) were ended by the Russian invasion of 1968. Pervasive Soviet control reinforces the hard line stance of the present regime.

Religion: The remarkable freedom of the 'Prague Spring' of 1968 has been replaced by increasing repression and persecution of the churches to almost Stalinist proportions. Since 1984, the Catholic leadership has taken a much stronger stance against the repressive policies of the authorities.

Non-religious/Atheist 21.3%. The Communists *claim* this to have been increased to 64%.

Jews 0.1% 4,000 left of the 360,000 in 1938.

Christian 78.6%.

   Roman Catholic 68%. 10,540,000a. Only 1 million attend church regularly.

   Other Catholic 3.2%. 501,000a. Mainly the Czech Hussite Church which broke away from Rome in 1920.

Orthodox 1.2% 181,000a.
Protestant 6%. 935,000a: 570,000m. Denominations 16. Largest
(adult members):

Slovak Evang. Lutheran Church		300,000
Slovak Reformed Church	est.	100,000
Evang. Church of Czech Brethren		78,200
United Methodist Church		10,000
Moravian Church		9,700
Seventh Day Adventist Church		7,800
Church of Brethren (Congreg.)		6,000
Brethren	est.	5,400
Pentecostal Church (AoG)		4,600
Baptist Church		4,100

Evangelical 2.1% of population.

ROMANIA

Romania is slightly smaller than the United Kingdom. It lies half way between the equator and the north pole and has a temperate climate. The River Danube meanders through the flat plains to the Black Sea while the Carpathian Mountains and the Transylvanian Alps provide refuge for a wide variety of wild animals.

A characteristic Romanian dish is drob de miel, *a fried calf's stomach with boiled lamb's liver, lungs and heart, which is chopped and mixed with eggs and fat. This is said to be highly nutritious! Another local dish is* sarmale, *minced meat rolled in pickled cabbage leaves. Western cuisine is sometimes available in large restaurants and tourist hotels.*

Area 237,000 sq.km. Area is much reduced by Russian seizure of Bessarabia in 1940 (now the Moldavian Soviet Socialist Republic).
Population 22,800,000. Annual growth 0.9%. People per sq.km. 96.
Peoples
Romanian 84%. A Latin people descended from Romans settled in Dacia.
Hungarian 8.5%. In Transylvania.
Minorities 7.5%. Gypsy 700,000; German 300,000; Jew 106,000; Turk 100,000; Ukrainian 67,000; Serbian 65,000; etc.
Literacy 98%. Official languages: Romanian, Hungarian.
Capital: Bucharest 2,200,000. Urbanization 49%.
Economy: Rigid centralized control has nullified benefit of economic links with the West, and Romania is now Europe's poorest nation with a steady deterioration in 1981–83.

Politics: Communist coup in 1947 with Russian support. The very harsh and repressive Communist regime had followed a nationalistic, independent line since 1963.

Religion: The registered churches are very strictly controlled. Many evangelical believers are forced to worship in illegal groups because the government rarely allows the registration of new churches. Persecution of churches is the most severe of any of the Eastern European states.

Non-religious/Atheist 14%.

Muslim 1.2%. Predominantly Turks, some Bulgars and Gypsies.

Jews 0.5%. Steadily declining through emigration to Israel.

Christian 84.2%.

    Orthodox 67.4%; 15,400,000a 10,700,000m. Denominations 6.

    Largest (adherents):

Romanian Orthodox Church	12,200,000

    Roman Catholic 5.5%. 1,244,000a 900,000m.

    Marginal groups 0.3%. 66,000a 48,000m.

    Protestant 11%. 2,500,000a; 1,500,000m. Denominations 14 legally acknowledged. Largest (adult members):

Reformed Church		520,000
Baptist Union	(?)	340,000
Church of God		230,000
Assemblies of God		170,000
Lutheran Church		94,500
Brethren	(?)	63,000
Seventh Day Adventist Church		57,000

    Evangelical 7.8% of population (11% if the Lord's Army Christians are included).

YUGOSLAVIA

Yugoslavia is the largest of the Balkan countries and varies greatly in culture, scenery and climate. The many peoples— Slovenians, Serbs, Croatians, Montenegrins, Herzegovinians, Bosnians and Macedonians—all work together but preserve their individual customs and culture. The climate varies from the Mediterranean on the coast to greater extremes of hot and cold inland. In the southern part of Yugoslavia the cyrillic script is used more than the latin letters.

Yugoslav cooking incorporates features of both oriental and european cookery. Tea is served with lemon or rum. Coffee in the south is normally black (Turska kava) but can also be ordered white (bijela kava). National dishes include cevapcici, *meat rolls (small); and* raznijici, *small pieces of pork roasted on spits, usually served with salt and huge chunks of crusty white bread.*

Area 256,000 sq.km. A Balkan state bordering on the Adriatic Sea.
Population 23,100,000. Annual growth ¢0.7%. People per sq.km. 90.
Peoples
Serbo-Croatian-speaking 70%. Four distinct Slavic peoples:
  Serbian 39.4%. Predominant in centre and east, and mainly
  Orthodox.
  Croatian 21%. Mainly in northwest and along Dalmation coast.
  Predominantly Catholic.
  Bosnian 6%. Serbian Muslims, but officially considered an ethnic
  entity in the central republic of Bosnia.
  Montenegrin 2.6%. Mainly in the south coastal republic of
  Montenegro.
Slovene 8%. A Slavic people in the northwestern republic of Slovenia.
Albanian 7.8%. Majority in the Kosovo region adjoining Albania and
many in Montenegro and Macedonia. Mainly Muslim; descendants of
the ancient Illyrians.
Macedonian 6%. A Slavic people related to the Bulgarians in the far
southern republic of Macedonia. Predominantly Orthodox.
Hungarian 2%. A large minority in Vojvodina region. Many are
Catholic or Reformed Protestant.
Other minorities 7.2%. Romany Gypsies, maybe 300,000; Rumelian
Turks 125,000; Bulgarians 36,000; Ukranians 30,000, etc.
Literacy 90%. Official languages: Serbo-Croatian, Slovene and
Macedonian and, locally, six other languages. All languages 20. Bible
translations 8Bi 3NT 3por.
Capital: Belgrade 1,600,000. Other major city: Zagreb 1,200,000.
Urbanization 37%.
Economy: The world recession in 1979 exposed the inbuilt weaknesses
of a bloated bureaucracy and excessive regionalization. There is a
massive international debt, much unemployment and high inflation.
The wide disparity in living standards between the wealthier north and
poor south has further strained the fragile unity of the state.
Politics: Modern Yugoslavia developed from fragments of the Austro-
Hungarian and Turkish Ottoman Empire between 1878 and 1918.
Communist republic formed in 1945, but non-aligned in world politics
since President Tito's break with the USSR in 1948. Communism has
not been so authoritarian as in other East European states. Yugoslavia is
a federal socialist state consisting of six republics, two autonomous
regions, three religions, eight major national groups and two alphabets!
The fragmented and fierce nationalism of the various ethnic groups
helped trigger off World War I, provoked intense civil war in World

War II, and poses a flash-point for possible future conflict. Since Tito's death a complex collective leadership and devolution of power to the constituent republics has barely managed to keep the country together, and has hampered development and economic reform. Croatian and Albanian nationalisms are the two most sensitive issues today.

Religion: Atheism is actively promoted by the state in the education system. There is considerable religious freedom, though active proselytization is discouraged. There are restrictions on churches' social and cultural ministries, and some discrimination against Christians in job opportunities.

Non-religious/Atheist 18%. The Communist party has 2,200,000 members.

Muslim 11%. Bosnians, 80% of Albanians, Gypsies, Turks. Most are Sunni Muslims, a few are Shi'a. There are 2,250 functioning mosques.

Christian 71%. Affiliated 67%. Many are baptized, but do not attend church.

Orthodox 36.7%. 8,480,000a. Denominations 7. Mainly Serbians and Macedonians, a few Albanians.

Roman Catholic 29.7%. 6,860,000a. Mainly Slovenes, Croats and Hungarians and some Albanians.

Protestant 0.7%. 162,000a; 96,000m. Denominations approx. 40.

Largest (adult members):

Lutheran Churches (3)	42,000
Reformed Church (Hungarian)	20,000
Pentecostal Churches (4)	11,300
Seventh Day Adventist Church	10,600
Baptist Church	3,650
Methodist Church (Macedonian & Hung)	1,850

Evangelicals 0.16% of population.

Foreign Christians serving Yugoslavians est. 25.

Missionaries from within Yugoslavia est. 10.

Statistics in small print reproduced with permission and taken from 'Operation World' published by STL.